Women's Suffrage

Other books in the History Firsthand series:

HISTORY
HF
FIRSTHAND

Women's Suffrage

Richard Haesly, *Book Editor*

Daniel Leone, *President*
Bonnie Szumski, *Publisher*
Scott Barbour, *Managing Editor*
David M. Haugen, *Series Editor*

GREENHAVEN
PRESS ®

THOMSON

GALE

San Diego • Detroit • New York • San Francisco • Cleveland
New Haven, Conn. • Waterville, Maine • London • Munich

For more information, contact
Greenhaven Press
27500 Drake Rd.
Farmington Hills, MI 48331-3535
Or you can visit our Internet site at http://www.gale.com

LIBRARY OF CONGRESS CATALOGING-IN-PUBLICATION DATA

Women's suffrage / Richard Haesly, book editor.
    p. cm. — (History firsthand)
    Includes bibliographical references and index.
    ISBN 0-7377-1305-4 (pbk. : alk. paper) — ISBN 0-7377-1304-6 (lib. : alk. paper)
    1. Women—Suffrage—United States—History. 2. Women in politics—United States—History. I. Haesly, Richard, 1969– . II. Series.
    JK1896 .W66 2003
    324.6'23'0973—dc21   2002023170

Contents

Chapter 2: Making a Case for National Women's Suffrage

the question of granting women the right to vote directly to the voters of New York State. She details the intricate—and sometimes amusing, but often frustrating—political maneuvers that she endured to convince key members of the legislature even to move the bill out of committee and onto the floor for a vote.

Ernest Bernbaum, a Harvard professor of literature and an avid opponent of women's suffrage, explains why he believes that Massachusetts failed to give women the right to vote in 1915. Although he offers several reasons, primary among them is the fact that most Massachusetts citizens disapproved of the tactics employed by the suffragists.

Chapter 4: The Nineteenth Amendment

In 1916, the president of the National American Woman Suffrage Association, Carrie Chapman Catt, details for her organization the steps necessary to encourage the proposal and ratification of a constitutional amendment granting women the right to vote. More than simply a civics lesson, however, Catt's overview of the process provided supporters of the cause with specific tasks that they must take to insure victory.

Maud Wood Park, the chairperson of the Congressional Committee of the National American Woman Suffrage Association, writes to the chair of each state-level suffrage organization, notifying them how NAWSA hopes to directly lobby members of Congress to secure passage of a women's suffrage amendment.

In a pamphlet designed to be a primer for suffragists across the country, Alice Stone Blackwell, the recording secretary of the National American Woman Suffrage Association, instructs readers on how to counter the major arguments against giving women the right to vote. Combining statistics, logical reasoning, and a healthy dose of humor, Blackwell provides a compelling overview of the common debates surrounding women's suffrage.

Foreword

In his preface to a book on the events leading to the Civil War, Stephen B. Oates, the historian and biographer of Abraham Lincoln, John Brown, and other noteworthy American historical figures, explained the difficulty of writing history in the traditional third-person voice of the biographer and historian. "The trouble, I realized, was the detached third-person voice," wrote Oates. "It seemed to wring all the life out of my characters and the antebellum era." Indeed, how can a historian, even one as prominent as Oates, compete with the eloquent voices of Daniel Webster, Abraham Lincoln, Harriet Beecher Stowe, Frederick Douglass, and Robert E. Lee?

Oates's comment notwithstanding, every student of history, professional and amateur alike, can name a score of excellent accounts written in the traditional third-person voice of the historian that bring to life an event or an era and the people who lived through it. In *Battle Cry of Freedom*, James M. McPherson vividly re-creates the American Civil War. Barbara Tuchman's *The Guns of August* captures in sharp detail the tensions in Europe that led to the outbreak of World War I. Taylor Branch's *Parting the Waters* provides a detailed and dramatic account of the American Civil Rights Movement. The study of history would be impossible without such guiding texts.

Nonetheless, Oates's comment makes a compelling point. Often the most convincing tellers of history are those who lived through the event, the eyewitnesses who recorded their firsthand experiences in autobiographies, speeches, memoirs, journals, and letters. The Greenhaven Press History Firsthand series presents history through the words of first-person narrators. Each text in this series captures a significant historical era or event—the American Civil War, the

Great Depression, the Holocaust, the Roaring Twenties, the 1960s, the Vietnam War. Readers will investigate these historical eras and events by examining primary-source documents, authored by chroniclers both famous and little known. The texts in the History Firsthand series comprise the celebrated and familiar words of the presidents, generals, and famous men and women of letters who recorded their impressions for posterity, as well as the statements of the ordinary people who struggled to understand the storm of events around them—the foot soldiers who fought the great battles and their loved ones back home, the men and women who waited on the breadlines, the college students who marched in protest.

The texts in this series are particularly suited to students beginning serious historical study. By examining these firsthand documents, novice historians can begin to form their own insights and conclusions about the historical era or event under investigation. To aid the student in that process, the texts in the History Firsthand series include introductions that provide an overview of the era or event, timelines, and bibliographies that point the serious student toward key historical works for further study.

The study of history commences with an examination of words—the testimony of witnesses who lived through an era or event and left for future generations the task of making sense of their accounts. The Greenhaven Press History Firsthand series invites the beginner historian to commence the process of historical investigation by focusing on the words of those individuals who made history by living through it and recording their experiences firsthand.

Introduction

On March 30, 1776, Abigail Adams wrote to her husband, John Adams, who was a delegate to the Continental Congress then drafting the Declaration of Independence. She asked him, as the founding fathers considered what sort of document they would write, "Remember the Ladies, and be more generous and favorable to them than your ancestors. . . . Remember all Men would be tyrants if they could. If particular care and attention is not paid to the Ladies we are determined to foment a Rebellion, and will not hold ourselves bound by any Laws in which we have no voice or Representation."[1] Despite this early concern by a prominent American woman, who would be the wife of the second president of the United States and the mother of the sixth president, no such rebellion took place. In fact, for the first one hundred years of the United States, American women had very few social, economic, or political rights. In most states women were not legally allowed to own property, and in many states women were constitutionally barred from voting in any election.

Although American women were forbidden to take an active role in many realms of social and political life, some changes were occurring that would eventually lead to vocal demands for change. Perhaps the greatest influence was economic progress, which increased the pressure for a more educated female workforce. In 1814 the first power-driven loom was established in Waltham, Massachusetts. This technological advance encouraged many women, who were proficient weavers since their education often (and only) stressed such handicrafts, to enter the workforce. Similarly, as the country's population grew, the demand for teachers—

one of the few jobs available to women—was also increasing. Both changes suggested that women beyond the upper class needed more extensive education. This education was first provided primarily by private institutions. However, as voting rights were gradually extended to all men over the age of twenty-one, regardless of property holdings, the need for public education grew in order to have educated voters. Because women did not have the right to vote, public education for women did not seem to be a pressing need. It was not until the Civil War that public high school education would be provided to women in cities such as Philadelphia and Boston.

Although the provision of public education for women would progress rather slowly, private institutions began to provide urban, middle-class women with access to new realms of ideas and education. Many of these women continued learning after they finished their formal education. They formed societies in which women would meet to sew but also to read "useful" books. At around the same time, particularly during the 1830s and 1840s, the abolitionist movement—the movement designed to abolish slavery in the United States—began to become more politically active. Several of the women's societies would discuss the issue of abolition since it was one of the most controversial of the day. Because it was considered unseemly for women to take part in such "manly" pursuits as speaking in front of mixed-gender crowds, participating in public debates, and discussing political issues, women would often organize their own anti-slavery societies. These organizations provided many women with important skills that would become extremely useful when they began to fight for women's suffrage. In fact, many of the first generation of suffragist leaders got their start in the abolitionist movement. Individuals such as Lucy Stone, Lucretia Mott, Frances Harper, Sojourner Truth, and Susan B. Anthony learned their public speaking and organizational skills from their participation in the abolitionist movement. Furthermore, it became clear to many women abolitionists that the arguments that they were developing in favor of freeing slaves applied equally well to the unequal treatment that all women received. Many women began to include in their antislavery speeches demands for women's rights, despite the protests of many male abolitionists who felt that mixing the message would alienate potential supporters.

Denied Participation Because of Their Gender

In 1840 the World Anti-Slavery Conference was held in London, England. William Lloyd Garrison, the editor of the Boston-based abolitionist newspaper the *Liberator*, had become the figurehead of the U.S. abolition movement. In fact, he used the support of female antislavery societies to take control of the American Anti-Slavery Society. Because of this, he selected a number of women to be part of the official American delegation to the London conference.

When they arrived in London after a long transatlantic boat trip, the female delegates were not allowed to take their seats because the convention organizers felt that women had no place in such a public, political forum. In fact, one of the men who objected to the women participating in the meeting was a black delegate who thought that including women would make the meeting less legitimate in the court of public opinion. A compromise was eventually struck whereby the women were allowed to watch the proceedings from an upper balcony in the meeting chamber, but this solution was hardly satisfactory. Garrison took his seat with the female delegates as a show of solidarity. Elizabeth Cady Stanton, one of the American women who was denied the ability to participate in the convention, described her reaction to this exclusion in her autobiography: "[Abolitionists] would have been horrified at the idea of burning the flesh of the distinguished women present with red-hot irons, but the crucifixion of their pride and self-respect, the humiliation of their spirit, seemed to them a most trifling matter."[2]

Stanton had attended the meeting with her husband, Henry, as part of their honeymoon. To have traveled so far and to be relegated to a passive observer made an indelible mark on Stanton and another female delegate, Lucretia Mott. These two women decided that a separate conference designed solely to discuss women's rights was needed. Although it took eight years before they could actually arrange a conference, historian Andrew Sinclair believes that their exclusion from the World Anti-Slavery Conference was a watershed moment in the history of American women's suffrage: "The rejection of women delegates was . . . vital for the organization of a political woman's movement *separate* from the anti-slavery movement. Nothing succeeds in raising a rival like exclusion. . . . The world convention was to prove more important in the history of those it kept out than of those it included."[3]

The Seneca Falls Convention and the Declaration of Sentiments

Although Lucretia Mott and Elizabeth Cady Stanton vowed to hold a conference on women's rights, it took eight years for them to carry through on their promise. Mott was an active woman. At age twenty-eight, she became an ordained minister in the Quaker church. Her job as a minister and a vocal opponent of slavery made it difficult for her to find time to plan the convention that she and Stanton wanted to hold. Stanton was also extremely busy. Her husband was also an active abolitionist, and his work took him all over the country. Sometimes Stanton would join him as he spoke to angry mobs about the need to ban slavery in the United States. Most of the time, however, she remained at home caring for their three children.

When the family lived in Boston, Stanton was able to combine her duties as a housewife with more political and intellectual pursuits. However, the Stanton family later moved to Seneca Falls, in upstate New York. This move would prove to be critical in the history of the women's rights movement. Life as a housewife in a small town began to wear down Stanton in a profound way. As she describes,

The general discontent I felt with woman's portion as wife,

mother, housekeeper, physician, and spiritual guide, the chaotic condition into which everything fell without her constant supervision, and the wearied, anxious look of the majority of women, impressed me with the strong feeling that some active measures should be taken to remedy the wrongs of society in general and of women in particular. My experiences at the World Anti-Slavery Convention, all I had read on the legal status of women, and the oppression I saw everywhere, together swept across my soul, intensified now by many personal experiences. It seemed as if all the elements had conspired to impel me to some onward step. I could not see what to do or where to begin—my only thought was a public meeting for protest and discussion.[4]

Thus, when Stanton spent the day with Mott, who was in central New York visiting friends, Stanton suggested that they fulfill the promise that they had made in London eight years earlier. These women sat around a mahogany table, which is now part of the Smithsonian museum in Washington, D.C., and wrote an announcement that they published in the local paper, the *Seneca County Courier*, on July 14, 1848. The announcement invited both men and women to attend a women's rights convention, which would be held in Seneca Falls, New York, on July 19 and 20, 1848. Only women were to attend on the first day, but both men and women were invited to attend the second day of the convention.

The two women decided that they wanted a declaration of some kind, upon which discussions at the convention could focus. Stanton had the responsibility for writing the document. She decided to base her Declaration of Sentiments on the Declaration of Independence to give her arguments a sense of history and also because she strongly believed that women's rights were implied by Thomas Jefferson's famous document. For example, Thomas Jefferson wrote, "All men are created equal." If one took this to mean humankind, as these abolitionists and budding suffragists interpreted it, then the Declaration of Independence declared that men and women alike share equal social and political rights. Also like the Declaration of Independence, Stanton's Declaration of Sentiments included a list of grievances that demonstrated that women had been socially, economically, and politically subjugated to men.

She then listed a number of rights that she believed women must have to ensure equality between the sexes. The list included economic, social, and political rights. Economically, she called for women to have the legal right to hold property. Social rights included the right of women to be allowed to speak their mind, to seek a higher level of education, and to be treated equally. The most controversial right that she declared was the political right of female enfranchisement, or the right for women to vote. Her husband, when he saw a draft of her declaration, vowed that he would not attend the meeting for fear that such a demand would derail the entire convention. Even her fellow convention planner, Lucretia Mott, believed that the call for women's suffrage was unnecessarily provocative. Only African American abolitionist Frederick Douglass, who lived in nearby Rochester, New York, supported the demand for women's suffrage.

In the end, Henry Stanton's and Lucretia Mott's worst fears were proven wrong, but not entirely. Henry Stanton remained true to his word and made sure that business took him out of town so that he could not attend the meeting. Elizabeth Cady Stanton's Declaration of Sentiments caused quite a stir as well as considerable discussion and debate among the one hundred men and women who eventually signed the document at the close of the convention. The most heated debates were around female enfranchisement, but those who attended accepted all of Stanton's original resolutions. However, the resolution that called for granting women the right to vote was the only one that did not pass unanimously.

The Declaration of Sentiments would serve as the touchstone for the women's rights movement in America for the remainder of the century. It also increased Stanton's prominence. One woman who asked to meet with Stanton was Susan B. Anthony. Anthony was active in the temperance movement that sought to decrease the perceived ill effects of alcohol on society. Anthony had been advocating radical women's rights, such as the right to vote and the ability to obtain a divorce, as part of the temperance cause. Anthony and Stanton saw each other as kindred spirits. After meeting in 1851, these two women began a collaboration that would last half a century.

The Civil War and Abolition

From 1861 to 1865, the United States became embroiled in a horrific war that divided the nation. Although scholars argue that the Civil War was not entirely based on slavery, the question of whether the United States should ban slavery throughout the country was an important issue. Because many suffragists remained active in the abolition movement—the issue that gave most women their start in political activism—women were hopeful that, when the North successfully defeated the South, slavery would indeed be abolished throughout the nation. The abolitionists soon achieved an important victory when, in 1865, the Thirteenth Amendment to the U.S. Constitution abolished slavery altogether.

Although freeing the slaves was an important first step, more needed to be done. The states of the Confederacy, although forced to abandon slavery, had no intention of providing the freed slaves with any real rights or freedoms. Thus, the abolition movement and leading northern politicians began discussing the need for a constitutional amendment that would grant the former slaves the rights of American citizenship. These citizenship protections would be put together into one of the most important constitutional amendments in American history, the Fourteenth Amendment.

The Fourteenth Amendment is complicated, but its impact remains extremely powerful to this day. Among other aspects, the Fourteenth Amendment created for the first time the idea of national citizenship. Section 1 reads, "All persons born or naturalized in the United States, and subject to the jurisdiction thereof, are citizens of the United States and of the State wherein they reside." The implication of this is that all of the slaves who had been freed by the Thirteenth Amendment would become citizens when the Fourteenth

Amendment was ratified. Furthermore, since no distinction is made between women and men, this section makes all people, regardless of gender, American citizens if they were born in the United States or if they are officially naturalized.

The Fourteenth Amendment also described what American citizenship provides all Americans. First, the equal protection clause of the Fourteenth Amendment says that all American citizens enjoy equal protection under the laws. Second, the due process clause describes that no state can "deprive any person of life, liberty, or property, without due process of law." Once again, these citizenship rights apply to all citizens, whether they were former slaves or free persons or if they were men or women.

Therefore, the Fourteenth Amendment provided important rights to all Americans. Many women hoped that the amendment would be a vehicle for their emancipation as much as it would be a way to increase the status of the freed slaves. Unfortunately, the Fourteenth Amendment also included clauses that made a distinction between men and women for the first time. Until the Fourteenth Amendment, the U.S. Constitution did not include the word *male* (or *female*). However, the Fourteenth Amendment wanted to ensure that the former states of the Confederacy would actually respect the citizenship rights that the amendment proposed. Thus, the amendment also threatened to punish any state that denied the right to vote to any "male inhabitant."

The Women's Suffrage Movement Divides

Elizabeth Cady Stanton and Susan B. Anthony at first hoped to combine the emancipation of the slaves with their demands for women's suffrage. The organization that they formed, the American Equal Rights Association (AERA), was designed to advocate for both simultaneously. During the debate of the Fourteenth Amendment in Congress, they urged that the clause including the three uses of the word *male* be removed from the amendment. Many male abolitionists, some of whom had been including calls for women's suffrage in their speeches during the 1850s, feared that a formal linking of these two causes would lead to a rejection of the amendment. They refused to express AERA's demands to the members of Congress when they met with them. Congress passed the Fourteenth Amendment with the word *male* included in June 1866. The amendment was ratified in 1868.

Women march in a suffrage parade to spark interest in and attract publicity for their cause.

In essence, abolitionist leaders asked the feminists to hold off on their concerns until protections for the freed slaves could be secured. At that point, the abolitionist movement could discuss separately the idea of women's suffrage. Some of the more conservative women, under the leadership of Henry Blackwell and Lucy Stone, accepted this and began campaigning for the ratification of the Fourteenth Amendment as it was proposed.

Anthony and Stanton, on the other hand, were unwilling to make their calls for women's suffrage secondary. They understood that many in the abolitionist movement would not become active in protests for women's suffrage because many of them did not actually believe that women should be allowed to vote. Suffragists sensed that, since the amendment process is so daunting, if women's suffrage was not included in the Fourteenth Amendment, it would be decades before the issue would be addressed again. Furthermore, the explicit extension of the right to vote to male former slaves in the Fifteenth Amendment meant that giving women the right to vote would require its own constitutional amendment or a separate law in each state legislature. Finally, there was a strong sense of betrayal. Anthony and Stanton had both been active members in the abolition movement. Then, when the moment came for the abolition movement to help advance the cause of women's rights—merely by eliminating the use of the word *male* in the Fourteenth Amendment—they were told that women's rights were simply not as critical as the rights of the freed (male) slaves.

The division between the two camps—those who were willing to deal with abolition first and then turn to women's suffrage, and those who refused to place women's rights on the back burner—would be one that would plague the movement for many decades. In 1869 the divide widened when Anthony and Stanton formed the National Woman Suffrage Association (NWSA). Later that year Blackwell and Stone formed a rival organization, the American Woman Suffrage Association (AWSA). These two organizations would remain separate, and oftentimes bitter enemies, until 1890, when they merged to form the National American Woman Suffrage Association (NAWSA).

More than a disagreement over tactics, the NWSA and the AWSA represented a number of differences. First, Anthony and Stanton's NWSA was much more politically liberal than the more conservative AWSA. Historian Andrew Sinclair reports, "Stanton declared that she would say amen to the Devil if he offered money for a [feminist] newspaper."[5] The NWSA was an organization that was dedicated to women's rights, not simply women's suffrage. Although securing the right to vote was seen as critical, the NWSA also advocated an extension of a wide array of social and economic rights. Many of the proposed rights were contentious, such as equal property rights and employment rights for women, and more conservative supporters of women's suffrage simply would not agree with them. The NWSA also allied itself with controversial figures such as Victoria Claflin Woodhull, the first woman to run for president (in 1872) and an advocate of "free love." Such notoriety probably lost the NWSA many potential supporters by seeming to link women's suffrage with ideas that very few in the late nineteenth century would support.

Finally, and most damaging, the NWSA unfortunately included a strand of racism that would harm the entire women's rights movements for decades. Despite their abolitionist backgrounds, Anthony and especially Stanton began to link support for women's suffrage as a counterbalance to the increasing rights for African Americans. As Ellen DuBois, the historian who compiled and analyzed the letters between Stanton and Anthony, argues,

> Political forces beyond their control had made it impossible to unite the demands of women and the freedmen, but Stanton and Anthony took the further step of opposing feminism to Black suffrage. On the one hand, they argued that white women, educated and virtuous, were more deserving of the vote than the ex-slaves. On the other hand, they attempted to build feminism on the basis of white women's racism. At times, Stanton even fueled white women's sexual fears of Black men to rouse them against Black suffrage and for their own enfranchisement. Stanton's appeals to such arguments peaked during the 1869 debate over the Fifteenth Amendment, which fully enfranchised Black men. After the Amendment's ratification, her outright racism subsided, but the more subtle habit of seeing women's grievances from the viewpoint of white women had been firmly established within the suffrage movement.[6]

Claiming Women's Suffrage

Advocates of women's suffrage used many different tactics to call attention to their cause. One that was employed by Anthony and other radical supporters of women's suffrage was to argue that women actually had the right to vote under the Fourteenth Amendment of the U.S. Constitution. Therefore, all they needed to do was to register to vote and cast their ballots.

Led by the example of Anthony, 150 women across the United States attempted to test this theory by registering and then voting in the 1872 presidential elections. Three women, one in New Hampshire and two in Michigan, actually had their votes counted in the 1872 elections. Most, however, were stopped by officials who refused to register them to vote since there were state laws against women voting.

Anthony was indicted when she voted in November 1872. She was taken to court, under the threat of a hefty five-hundred-dollar fine as well as up to three years in jail, for leading a group of sixteen women to vote. Although all of the women who went to the polls in Anthony's hometown of Rochester, New York, were charged with a crime, the case against Anthony was the primary trial of importance, given her leadership position in the feminist movement of the day. At her trial in June 1873, Anthony was found guilty and fined one hundred dollars. She steadfastly refused to pay the fine. The judge allowed the matter to drop, thereby denying Anthony's wish to pursue her case to the U.S. Supreme Court.

However, a second court case coming out of the 1872 presidential elections eventually reached the Supreme Court. A Missouri woman, Virginia Minor, sued the Missouri registrar, Reese Happersett, for refusing to allow her to register to vote. Minor claimed that Happersett had violated her right to vote under the Fourteenth Amendment. In 1875 the Supreme Court unanimously ruled in *Minor v. Happersett* that no part of the U.S. Constitution guaranteed women the right to vote, and that each state could determine the issue for itself. This was a crucial ruling, for it meant that women could only be granted the right to vote by amending the Constitution or by changing the law in every state.

How the West Was Won

While legal battles were taking place in the East, women in the West were actually winning the right to vote. In 1869 the Wyoming Territory became the first part of the United States to grant women the right to vote. And, when it joined the Union in 1890, Wyoming became the first state to grant women the right to vote. Colorado followed in 1893. Utah and Idaho did the same in 1896. However, a long period in which no states voted in favor of women's suffrage followed. It was not until 1910 that Washington enfranchised women, followed by California in 1911, and Arizona, Oregon, and Kansas in 1912.

Why did western states agree much earlier than the rest of the country to grant women the right to vote? In general, ideas about women in the West reflected those of the rest of the country. However, the smaller populations in the western states meant that prosuffrage activists had to convince a considerably smaller number of politicians to vote in favor of women's suffrage than was the case in the more populous states in the East. For example, because of its small size, it only took twelve individuals in the Wyoming legislature to enfranchise women.

The Women's Suffrage Movement Reunites but Flounders

In 1890 the division of the American suffrage movement between Anthony and Stanton's NWSA and Blackwell and Stone's AWSA ended when Stone's only daughter, Alice Stone Blackwell, successfully formed a new organization, the National American Woman Suffrage Association (NAWSA). As its name implied, this new organization was to be an equal merger of the two rival organizations. NAWSA's first two presidents were the NWSA leaders Stanton (1890–1892) and Anthony (1892–1900). In practice, however, NAWSA reflected the views of the more conservative AWSA. For example, NAWSA quickly dropped other feminist issues, such as divorce reform, women's property rights, and the legalization of prostitution, which the NWSA had pursued as part of a collection of women's rights issues. Instead, NAWSA adopted AWSA's approach of concentrating solely on women's suffrage.

NAWSA also made the decision to stop holding its yearly meeting in Washington, D.C., where delegates would have easier access to politicians, and began to hold every other

meeting in another city, where it would be easier for delegates from western states to attend. Anthony's fear that this
approach would allow Washington politicians to ignore the
issue of women's suffrage proved correct. Once NAWSA reduced the frequency of its Washington meetings to every
other year, Congress failed to issue any favorable reports on
the issue of women's suffrage from 1893 until 1913.

Although uniting the two competing women's suffrage
organizations was an important step forward, NAWSA was
not an overnight success. As Eleanor Flexnor documents,
"From 1870 to 1910, there were 480 campaigns in thirty-
three states, just to get the issue submitted to the voters, of
which only seventeen resulted in actual referendum votes.
. . . Only two referenda were successful."[7] NAWSA perpet-
ually struggled to raise funds sufficient to run all of its various campaigns. As historian Sara Hunter Graham describes,
"Without a solid financial base to support organizers and
state campaigns, the movement would continue on the slow
path of gradualism and frustration."[8] An added obstacle was
the fact that although it called itself a national organization,
NAWSA relied heavily on each state organization to do
much of the actual work. Many of these state organizations
were poorly organized and politically ineffective. Thus, for
several decades successes in the battle for women's suffrage
were extremely sparse.

A Changing Tide

Although for many years the newly reunited women's suffrage movement could not point to any significant victories,
things began to change during the second decade of the
twentieth century. Much of this was due to the growth of the
Progressive Party throughout the country. The Progressives
believed that the citizens of the United States did not have
sufficient control over the politicians who were supposed to
be passing legislation on their behalf. Instead, they thought
that many legislatures were primarily interested in protecting important business interests, such as the liquor industry
in the western states and the railroads in California. Once

voters were able to put enough Progressive candidates into these state legislatures, new laws designed to increase greater democratic control were put into place. Many of the states in which the Progressives gained political power began to consider women's suffrage as a way of increasing democratic participation and control. The increasing number of politicians willing to debate the issue of women's suffrage would prove extremely helpful.

In 1913 the Illinois legislature voted to give women partial suffrage, allowing them to vote only in presidential elections. Illinois thus became the first state east of the Mississippi River to grant women the right to vote in any national or state election. As the number of states—and thus the number of members of Congress—willing to grant women suffrage increased, a national strategy to amend the Constitution seemed possible.

At the same time, newer members of the women's suffrage movement began pushing for more direct—and, in some cases, confrontational—tactics in support of the cause. Harriot Stanton Blatch, the daughter of Elizabeth Cady Stanton, had grown up in Britain, where she had learned tactics from the more militant British women's suffrage movement. When she returned to the United States, she established the Women's Political Union (WPU), which reached out more actively to working-class women who were entering the workforce in increasing numbers. She is also credited with organizing one of the more useful tools in the fight for women's suffrage, the suffrage parade. Although the first suffrage parade held in New York City in 1910 caused an uproar and outrage, it also grabbed publicity for the cause.

Alice Paul, who also spent three years in Britain, similarly used a parade to spark public interest in women's suffrage. In March 1913, Paul and a small group of more militant supporters organized a women's suffrage parade. This parade is often credited with making a constitutional amendment granting women's suffrage a political reality rather than simply a hope based on the slowly increasing number of states that had given women the right to vote.

The 1913 parade attracted nearly five thousand participants from throughout the country, including a handful of pro–women's suffrage congressmen. As Eleanor Flexnor recounts,

> With that dramatic sense which always characterized her suffrage work, Miss Paul chose the day before Woodrow Wilson's inauguration, since Washington would be filled with visitors from all over the country. When Mr. Wilson reached Washington and found the streets bare of any welcoming crowds, he is said to have asked where the people were; he was told they were over on Pennsylvania Avenue, watching the woman suffrage parade.[9]

Based on her experiences in Britain, Alice Paul had wisely obtained a permit in advance for the parade. This permit required the Washington, D.C., police to protect the parade participants should the crowd attempt to disrupt the parade in any way. The women's suffrage parade faced an often-hostile crowd that jeered and sometimes attempted to block the parade from moving forward. The police not only did nothing to stop the crowd, but there were also widespread accounts that members of the police actively participated in the taunting and harassment. Public outcry over the treatment of the parade participants was significant enough that official hearings were held in Congress, which legally oversees the running of the District of Columbia. Although the police officers were not found to be in dereliction of their duties, the sympathy that the women's suffrage movement gained, in the public and in Congress, placed the consideration of a constitutional amendment back on the political agenda.

Developing a "Winning Plan"

If the women's suffrage movement hoped to achieve passage and ratification of a constitutional amendment, it would need to become more united than ever before. The actual wording of the amendment was not an issue. Ever since 1878, when Senator Aaron Sargent of California introduced an amendment that provided for equal suffrage for men and women, the amendment for which the suffrage movement fought always read the same: "The right of citizens of the

United States to vote shall not be denied or abridged by the United States or any state on account of sex." This amendment was often referred to as the Anthony Amendment, in honor of Susan B. Anthony, who was Senator Sargent's close friend. Yet despite a clearly defined objective, the movement was troubled.

The women's suffrage movement was poorly organized and short of cash. In 1916 it selected a new president, Carrie Chapman Catt, who had served as president of NAWSA from 1900 until 1904. Catt was selected because the organization needed a president with vision, organization, and innovation—all of which would be needed for the final push to gain women's suffrage through a constitutional amendment. Catt took over the presidency of NAWSA in 1915. Three months later she called together the members of the executive council and presented to them what has become known as her Winning Plan.

The Winning Plan laid out a set of specific suggestions that she believed would lead to successful passage and ratification of the Anthony Amendment. First, NAWSA needed at least thirty-six state suffrage branches—the number of states that would be needed to ratify the constitutional amendment—that would willingly coordinate their efforts with the national organization. Their primary emphasis would be to convince Congress to propose the Nineteenth Amendment. This would require those states that already had women's suffrage to remind their politicians in Washington that women were an important political force. Some states, in which passage seemed likely, could attempt to get amendments to their state constitutions to increase the number of states with women's suffrage. However, those states where the national organization felt the cause was unlikely to be successful would have to postpone any state efforts and concentrate instead on the national strategy. She believed that if the state-level branches committed themselves to her plan, women would be granted the right to vote by 1922. It turned out, however, that it would take only four years for the Nineteenth Amendment to be proposed and ratified, largely because

NAWSA adopted nearly all of Catt's Winning Plan. Flexnor summarizes Catt's contribution in the following terms:

> It was Mrs. Catt's unique contribution to the achievement of greater democratic opportunities for American women that she was able to weld so many . . . seemingly disparate elements into a potent political force. Her greatest gift, outranking even her excellence as an organizer, was the statesmanlike vision which enabled her to conceive a plan and thus help to achieve the desired goal. . . . Such was the caliber of her leadership that it is no overstatement to say that Carrie Chapman Catt stands besides Miss [Susan B.] Anthony and Mrs. [Elizabeth Cady] Stanton in stature.[10]

Protests and Prison

Not every member of the women's suffrage movement signed on to the Winning Plan. The most notable breaks were made by Alice Paul and her National Woman's Party (NWP). The NWP agreed that a constitutional amendment was the appropriate goal; however, it disagreed over the tactics that should be undertaken to achieve the outcome. Some of this was probably based on the fact that the NWP was founded by more militant members of the women's suffrage movement who believed in direct confrontation strategies. In fact, the NWP had its origins in NAWSA's Congressional Union, but Paul had soon grown frustrated with NAWSA's conservative approach and forged her own organization.

Whereas NAWSA's Winning Plan called for supporters of women's suffrage to work with politicians in hopes of gaining their support, the NWP vowed to defeat politicians of any party that did not favor women's suffrage. One of their primary targets was Woodrow Wilson, whom they felt had not done enough to lead his Democratic Party in favor of women's suffrage. They promised to campaign against him in those states in which women had the right to vote in presidential elections. NAWSA saw these tactics as overly confrontational and ultimately ineffective. NAWSA distanced itself from the NWP and its increasingly attack-oriented approaches.

NAWSA and the NWP also disagreed over which tactics

were appropriate during an international crisis. World War I had been raging in Europe since 1914. Although the United States had avoided being drawn into the war for three years, by April 1917 it officially entered the war in defense of the Triple Alliance of Britain, France, and Russia. Although NAWSA still emphasized the need for a women's suffrage amendment, it did not wish to alienate potential support, from the public or from politicians, by pursuing their goals too aggressively. The same could not be said for the National Woman's Party. Starting in early 1917, the NWP started a new campaign of picketing the White House. Some of the banners hoped to link the democratic ideals that Wilson would eventually use to justify U.S. entry into the war. For example, banners proclaimed, "Democracy Begins at Home." Others were more derogatory. One sign referred to President Wilson as "Kaiser Wilson," an unflattering comparison to the German enemy.

At first, President Wilson seemed amused by the pickets. However, his mood changed when the United States actually entered the war. He became outraged at what he felt were unpatriotic acts that should be suspended during a time of national crisis. On June 22, 1917, Wilson ordered that the women be arrested. The only official charge that they faced was obstructing traffic outside of the White House. The courts tended to dismiss the first few cases that were brought. However, as the protests and arrests continued, they began to sentence the women to jail—first for a few days, but eventually they increased the sentence to as much as six months. In all, 218 women were arrested, and ninety-six were sent to prison.

The conditions that the women faced in the Occoquan, Virginia, workhouse and the District of Columbia jail were horrendous. The imprisoned women complained of unsanitary conditions, spoiled food, and beatings by other prisoners sanctioned by the warden and the guards. Several of the women protested their arrest and imprisonment by going on hunger strikes in order to gain more attention for their treatment. Many of these women were brutally force fed by the guards.

The arrests finally ended in November 1917. In March 1918 all of the women had their sentences overturned by the Court of Appeals. The overall impact of these protests remains a point of controversy to this day. Some claim that the publicity that was created by the pickets, their arrests, the deplorable conditions of their imprisonment, and their eventual release helped to force Congress to take seriously their demands for action on a constitutional amendment. Others, however, believe that their militant stance, especially during the early stages of American entrance into World War I, did more harm than good by alienating members of Congress who might have agreed with their goals but disagreed vehemently with their tactics.

The Nineteenth Amendment Is Proposed

On January 10, 1918, the House of Representatives met to debate the merits of proposing the Nineteenth Amendment, which would give women the same voting rights as men. NAWSA had been pursuing a campaign designed to gain as many votes in favor of the amendment as possible. NAWSA's Front Door Lobby, headed by Maud Wood Park, met with various congressmen to determine what level of support the amendment had. Her informal polls of the House of Representatives indicated that enough support existed to overcome the rather daunting two-thirds majority required to propose a constitutional amendment. However, there was no margin for error so the suffragists redoubled their efforts to avoid a costly setback by losing the vote by only a few votes. On the day of the vote, four of the members of the House who supported women's suffrage were extremely ill, but they made it to the floor to cast their votes. One had a broken arm and refused to have it set for fear that he would miss the vote; another came from a Baltimore hospital, where he had been for the past six months; and one was carried in on a stretcher for the final roll-call vote. The House of Representatives successfully passed the amendment by a vote of 274 to 136, precisely the number of votes that was needed for a two-thirds majority.

The members of the women's movement who were in the gallery observing the debate celebrated by cheering and singing. They could not celebrate their victory for long, however, since the amendment also needed passage by the Senate. This was actually the more obstinate of the two houses of Congress. Although many senators, especially those from southern states, opposed the amendment because they felt that it was "unladylike" for women to vote, many others did not wish to pass the amendment because they felt it violated the rights of each state to decide whether it wanted women to vote.

The Senate waited several months before it even took up the amendment that was passed by the House. Finally, in September 1918, the Senate began debating the Nineteenth Amendment. Based on informal polling of the senators, it seemed the amendment would face certain defeat unless extraordinary measures were taken. President Wilson took such measures, and in the process, he became the first president to directly address Congress in an attempt to convince its members to support a constitutional amendment. Wilson hoped that linking women's suffrage to the idea of democracy upon which American involvement in World War I had been based and using his position as the leader of the Democratic Party to convince uncertain Senate Democrats would give the amendment the few votes that it needed to clear the Senate. If that was the desired effect, President Wilson and the women's movement were soon disappointed. After Wilson's speech it became clear that many of the senators were primarily concerned with intervention by the federal government into something that ultimately should be the decision of each state. Furthermore, many senators resented the president's attempt to influence a decision, which the U.S. Constitution explicitly gave only to the legislature. The Senate rejected the amendment when it failed to achieve the necessary two-thirds majority.

Elections were held in November 1918, and several key senators who had opposed passage of the amendment were defeated or retired from office. Thus, the movement decided to press again for reconsideration of the Nineteenth Amendment. On May 20, 1919, the newly inaugurated House of Representatives overwhelmingly passed the amendment by a vote of 304 to 89. A few weeks later, on June 4, 1919, the Senate also approved the amendment by a two-thirds majority. The Nineteenth Amendment had been officially proposed. All that remained was ratification of the amendment by thirty-six states.

Ratification of the Nineteenth Amendment

The ratification process did not take long. In little over one year the thirty-sixth state ratified the Nineteenth Amendment. However, some scholars believe that the ratification debates posed a particularly important challenge to the women's suffrage movement. Historian Sara Hunter Graham writes,

> To many readers, ratification by the states seems almost an afterthought, easily accomplished after the gripping congressional drama was played out. In fact, this was far from true. Arguably, ratification was the most difficult political test NAWSA activists would face. . . . For the amendment to take effect, it had to be approved by thirty-six state legislatures; in each state, suffragists had to grapple with different political agendas, coalitions and personalities.[11]

Despite these challenges, NAWSA was well prepared for the battle, in no small part because Carrie Chapman Catt had anticipated these battles when she drew up her Winning Plan of 1916. One unexpected delay was that many of the states that had already granted women the right to vote did not ratify the federal amendment as quickly as one might have imagined. They eventually did agree to ratify the amendment, however, so their delay was really only an irritant rather than a serious obstacle.

By early 1920 NAWSA was confident enough to declare, in what it called its Victory Convention, that the Nineteenth Amendment would be successfully ratified by thirty-six states. The question was no longer *if* there was to be women's suffrage; rather, the question was *when* it would officially be instituted. The question was answered in August 1920 when Harry Burn, Tennessee's youngest legislator, received a note from his mother. Tennessee, if it voted in favor of the amendment, would become the thirty-sixth state to ratify it. Burn's mother, an ardent suffragist, asked her son to vote favorably for the amendment. Burn did not let his mother down. When the time came to cast his vote, he voted in favor of the amendment, helping to ensure that it would pass the Tennessee legislature by a slim two-vote majority.

With this vote, the Nineteenth Amendment was ratified. Women, after a battle that had lasted for decades—which took men and women across the country making countless speeches, participating in numerous debates, marching in parades, picketing the White House, subjecting themselves to ridicule, suffering great indignities, and even facing prison—were now allowed to vote in every election and in every state in the Union. Although they still faced a number of battles in their fight for social, economic, and political equality, women finally had an important political tool to help them achieve those other important rights.

Notes

1. Quoted in Nancy McGlen et al., *Women, Politics, and American Society.* 3rd ed. New York: Longman, 2002, p. 1.
2. Quoted in Andrew Sinclair, *The Emancipation of the American Woman.* New York: Harper and Row, 1966, p. 57.
3. Sinclair, *The Emancipation of the American Woman,* p. 57.
4. Quoted in Eleanor Flexnor, *Century of Struggle: The Woman's Rights Movement in the United States.* New York: Atheneum, 1972, pp. 73–74.
5. Sinclair, *The Emancipation of the American Woman,* p. 189.
6. Ellen DuBois, *The Elizabeth Cady Stanton–Susan B. Anthony Reader.* Boston: Northeastern University Press, 1992, p. 92.
7. Flexnor, *Century of Struggle,* p. 222.
8. Sara Hunter Graham, *Woman Suffrage and the New Democracy.* New Haven, CT: Yale University Press, 1996, p. 8.
9. Flexnor, *Century of Struggle,* p. 263.
10. Flexnor, *Century of Struggle,* p. 275.
11. Graham, *Woman Suffrage and the New Democracy,* p. 128.

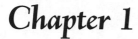

Chapter 1

The Movement
Begins

Chapter Preface

A religious revival in the mid-1800s encouraged men and women alike to take direct action in their daily lives to make life better for those less fortunate than themselves. Responses to this call included the establishment of the temperance movement (designed to control alcohol consumption) and the abolitionist movement (the fight to end slavery). These political campaigns are often cited as critical precursors to the struggle for women's suffrage because, unlike in other political arenas, women were able to take active and leading roles in both causes.

Women throughout the United States formed local and national female temperance and antislavery societies. These groups were often organized by and for women alone since American society still looked askance at women being too actively involved in the "male" pursuit of politics. In addition to their contribution to the broader movements, these female organizations brought together for the first time many women, who began to see that their gender as a whole suffered from many forms of discrimination. Some women in these groups began to link their concerns about the proper role of women in American society with the ideas of the abolition movement. For example, just as slaves were being denied the freedom on which America was supposedly based (the declaration that "All men are created equal"), some women observed that they too were being oppressed. In many ways, their situation was similar to the fate suffered by the slaves. Early suffragists explicitly stated this relationship in the abolitionist speeches that they gave around the country. In addition, through their active participation in the abolitionist and temperance movements, many early leaders of the women's suffrage movement learned and honed important political and leadership skills, such as how to organize a meeting, how to recruit members for the organization, how to raise money for their cause, and how to speak and debate in public. All of these skills would be put to the test as women often faced crowds extremely hostile to the idea that women should have the right to vote or even to the idea that women had the right to campaign for women's suffrage.

Women Should Be Involved in Politics

Susan T. Smith

Many women, despite the fact that they did not have the right to vote, became actively involved in the abolitionist movement. These experiences would provide these women with the excitement of political debate as well as the frustration of not being able to influence politics through voting. In May 1838, the Anti-Slavery Convention of Women was held in Philadelphia. Held in the city where the Declaration of Independence was signed, the convention was attended by a large number of men and women, both black and white. The combination of women actively participating in a political process and blacks attending the same conference with whites (especially white women) caused considerable protest. Throughout the convention, an angry mob could be heard attempting to disrupt the orators speaking out against slavery. In the end, the mob became so unruly that it burned down the Pennsylvania Hall, where the convention was taking place. Luckily, the conference had finished, and no one was injured.

One speaker, Susan T. Smith, gave the following address. In it, she rejects the notion that women should not be involved in the abolitionist movement because it is unseemly for women to be involved in politics. Instead she argues that women as well as men have an interest in the welfare of their country. Therefore, women should do whatever they can to rid the United States of such a morally repugnant institution as slavery. Finding a political voice in the debate over slavery gave women like Smith valuable experience that they could carry over into the fight for women's suffrage.

Excerpted from *History of Woman Suffrage*, vol. 1, edited by Elizabeth Cady Stanton, Susan B. Anthony, and Matilda Joslyn Gage (Rochester, NY: Charles Mann, 1889).

Dear Friends:—In that love for our cause which knows not the fear of man, we address you in confidence that our motives will be understood and regarded. We fear not censure from you for going beyond the circle which has been drawn around us by physical force, by mental usurpation, by the usages of ages; not any one of which can we admit gives the right to prescribe it; else might the monarchs of the old world sit firmly on their thrones, the nobility of Europe lord it over the man of low degree, and the chains we are now seeking to break, continue riveted on the neck of the slave. Our faith goes not back to the wigwam of the savage, or the castle of the feudal chief, but would rather soar with hope to that period when "right alone shall make might"; when the truncheon and the sword shall lie useless; when the intellect and heart shall speak and be obeyed; when "He alone whose right it is shall rule and reign in the hearts of the children of men."

Liberty or Slavery

We are told that it is not within "the province of woman" to discuss the subject of slavery; that it is a "political question," and that we are "stepping out of our sphere" when we take part in its discussion. It is not true that it is merely a political question; it is likewise a question of justice, of humanity, of morality, of religion; a question which, while it involves considerations of immense importance to the welfare and prosperity of our country, enters deeply into the home—concerns the every-day feelings of millions of our fellow beings. Whether the laborer shall receive the reward of his labor, or be driven daily to unrequited toil: whether he shall walk erect in the dignity of conscious manhood, or be reckoned among the beasts which perish; whether his bones and sinews shall be his own, or another's; whether his child shall receive the protection of its natural guardian, or be ranked among the live-stock of the estate, to be disposed of as the caprice or interest of the master may dictate; whether the sum of knowledge shall irradiate the hut of the peasant, or the murky cloud of ignorance brood darkly over it; whether "every one shall have the liberty to worship God according to the dictates of his own conscience," or man assume the prerogative of Jehovah and impiously seek to plant himself upon the throne of the Almighty. These considerations are all involved in the question of liberty or slavery.

And is a subject comprehending interests of such magnitude, merely a "political question," and one in which woman "can take no part without losing something of the modesty and gentleness which are her most appropriate ornaments"? May not the "ornament of a meek and quiet spirit" exist with an upright mind and enlightened intellect? Must woman necessarily be less gentle because her heart is open to the claims of humanity, or less modest because she feels for the degradation of her enslaved sisters, and would stretch forth her hand for their rescue?

By the Constitution of the United States, the whole physical power of the North is pledged for the suppression of domestic insurrections; and should the slaves maddened by oppression endeavor to shake off the yoke of the task-master, the men of the North are bound to make common cause with the tyrant, to put down at the point of the bayonet every effort on the part of the slave for the attainment of his freedom. And when the father, husband, son, and brother shall have left their homes to mingle in the unholy warfare; "to become the executioners of their brethren, or to fall themselves by their hands," will the mother, wife, daughter, and sister feel that they have no interest in this subject? Will it be easy to convince them that it is no concern of theirs, that their homes are rendered desolate and their habitations the abodes of wretchedness? Surely this consideration is of itself sufficient to arouse the slumbering energies of woman, for the overthrow of a system which thus threatens to lay in ruins the fabric of her domestic happiness; and she will not be deterred from the performance of her duty to herself, her family, and her country, by the cry of "political question."

Our Country's Interest Is Our Interest

But, admitting it to be a political question, have we no interest in the welfare of our country? May we not permit a thought to stray beyond the narrow limits of our own family circle and of the present hour? May we not breathe a sigh over the miseries of our countrywomen nor utter a word of remonstrance against the unjust laws that are crushing them to the earth? Must we witness "the headlong rage of heedless folly" with which our nation is rushing onward to destruction, and not seek to arrest its downward course? Shall we silently behold the land which we love with all the heart-warm affection of children, rendered a hissing and a reproach throughout the world by the system which is already "tolling the death-knell of her decease among the nations"?

No; the events of the last two years have "cast their dark shadows before," overclouding the bright prospects of the future, and shrouding our country in more than midnight gloom; and we can not remain inactive. Our country is as dear to us as to the proudest statesman; and the more closely our hearts cling to "our altars and our homes," the more fervent are our aspirations, that every inhabitant of our land may be protected in his fireside enjoyments by just and equal laws; that the foot of the tyrant may no longer invade the domestic sanctuary, nor his hand tear asunder those whom God himself has united by the most holy ties.

Let our course then still be onward! Justice, humanity, patriotism; every high and every holy motive urge us forward, and we dare not refuse to obey. The way of duty lies open before us, and though no pillar of fire be visible to the outward sense, yet an unerring light shall illumine our pathway, guiding us through the sea of persecution and the wilderness of prejudice and error, to the promised land of freedom, where "every man shall sit under his own vine and fig-tree, and none shall make him afraid."

Resolutions of the Seneca Falls Convention

Various Attendees

In July 1848, over three hundred people met in Seneca Falls, New York, to debate women's rights. The convention was organized by Elizabeth Cady Stanton and Lucretia Mott, both of whom had been denied admittance to the World Anti-Slavery Convention held in London in 1840, simply because they were women. This discrimination spurred these women to hold a convention with the primary goal of debating and ratifying a list of requirements to achieve women's rights. Based on the Declaration of Independence, Stanton and Mott's "Declaration of Sentiments and Resolutions" lists a wide array of changes that need to be made in American society to secure adequate women's rights. Primary among this list of demands was the right to vote. During the convention, it was this demand that caused the most controversy and was the only part of the resolution that did not pass unanimously by those attending the convention.

A my Post called the meeting to order and stated that at a preliminary meeting, held the previous evening at Protection Hall, herself, Sarah D. Fish and Rhoda De Garmo, were appointed a Committee to Nominate Officers for this Convention, and that they had concluded to propose the following names: *President*—Abigail Bush; *Vice-President*—

Excerpted from *Report of the Woman's Rights Convention, Held at Seneca Falls, N.Y., July 19th & 20th, 1848* (Rochester, NY: John Dick, 1848).

Laura Murray; *Secretaries*—Elizabeth McClintock, Sarah L. Hallowell and Catharine A.F. Stebbins.

The report of the committee was unanimously adopted by the Convention, excepting the case of Elizabeth McClintock, who declined accepting the office, on the ground of being unprepared to have a woman the presiding officer, therefore, she proposed the name of Mary H. Hallowell in her place, which being seconded by Mary Ann McClintock, she was duly appointed. To our great surprise, two or three other women—glorious reformers, well deserving the name— coming from a distance to attend the meeting, at first refused to take their seats upon the platform, or otherwise co-operate with the Convention, for the same cause. But as the meeting procccdcd, and thcy had listened to some opening remarks from our gentle but heroic President, their fears for the honor of the Convention subsided, after which they worked nobly for the cause that had called us together, and the meeting proceeded harmoniously to the end. . . .

The minutes of the preliminary meeting were then read by SARAH L. HALLOWELL, at which time much anxiety was manifested concerning the low voices of the women, and whenever reading or speaking was attempted, without giving time for adapting the voice to the size of the house, cries of "louder," "louder," nearly drowned every other sound, when the President arose and said:

"Friends, we present ourselves here before you, as an oppressed class, with trembling frames and faltering tongues, and we do not expect to be able to speak so as to be heard by all at first, but we trust we shall have the sympathy of the audience, and that you will bear with our weakness, now in the infancy of the movement. Our trust in the omnipotency of right is our only faith that we shall succeed."

WILLIAM C. NELL then read an eloquent address, highly commendatory of the energies and rare devotion of woman in every good cause, illustrated by facts in proof of her equality with man; adding that he should never cease to award the grateful homage of his heart for their zeal in behalf of the oppressed class with which he stood identified.

Equality, Not Superiority, of Women

Lucretia Mott arose and said, that although she was grateful for the eloquent speech just given, she must be allowed to object to some portions of it; such as styling "woman the better half of creation, and man a tyrant." Man had become so accustomed to speak of woman in the language of flattering compliments, that he indulges in such expressions unawares. She said that man was not a tyrant by nature, but had been made tyrannical by the power which had, by general consent, been conferred upon him; she merely wished that woman might be entitled to equal rights, and acknowledged as the equal of man, not his superior. Woman is equally tyrannical when she has irresponsible power, and we shall never place her in a true position, until we have formed a just estimate of mankind as created by God. . . .

ELIZABETH CADY STANTON then read the Declaration of Rights, which had been adopted by the Woman's Rights Convention held at Seneca Falls, which was cordially adopted by the meeting.

An expression of sentiment upon this Declaration of Rights being invited by the President, Mrs. Stanton expressed a hope that the invitation would be accepted. That if there were any present who did not agree with them in their notions of the Rights of Woman, that they would then and there make their objections, and not as at Seneca Falls, keep silent through all our deliberations, and afterwards, on the Sabbath day, use the pulpit throughout the town to denounce them, where they could not, of course, be allowed to reply.

Hereupon a Mr. Colton, of Connecticut, spoke freely of his great interest in the cause of woman. He loved the ladies as well as they loved themselves, but he would not have woman excel her proper sphere. He thought her place was at home, instead of engaging in the strife and contention of the political world. Home was her empire and her throne, and he should deprecate exceedingly her occupying the pulpit.

LUCRETIA MOTT replied in a speech of great sarcasm and eloquence. She said that the gentleman from New Haven had objected to woman occupying the pulpit, and indeed she could scarcely see how any one educated in New Haven, Ct., could think otherwise than he did. She said, we had all got our notions too much from the clergy, instead of the Bible. The Bible, she contended, had none of the prohibitions in regard to woman; and spoke of the "honorable women, not a few," etc., and desired Mr. Colton to read his Bible over again, and see if there was anything there to prohibit woman from being a religious teacher. . . .

Debate over a Woman's Right to Vote

Hon. WILLIAM C. BLOSS next spoke. He seemed disposed to allow all the privileges asked for by the women, except the elective franchise, and even that he almost admitted that good would result from; but he portrayed many obstacles in the path of that reform. He inquired if there was not a natural disqualification? Did not boys and girls exhibit dissimilar taste in the choice of playthings? The one preferring the noisy hammer, or the hoop, while the other, the darling doll at home? And were not these same traits carried out and more fully developed in after life? And he doubted if the ladies would use the right, if it were conferred upon them.

MILO D. CODDING also objected to that part of the Declaration which advocated woman's right to the elective franchise. He thought it sufficient for woman to vote through her father, brothers, or husband, but he finally concluded by wishing her a hearty God speed in her enterprise.

FREDERICK DOUGLASS followed in an eloquent and argumentative appeal for Woman's Rights, replying in a clear and conclusive manner to the gentleman who had spoken on the other side. He thought that the true basis of rights was the capacity of individuals; and as for himself, he should not dare claim a right that he would not concede to woman. As to the enfranchisement of woman, it need not be questioned whether she would use that right or not; man had no right to withhold it from her. . . .

At the close of Frederick Douglass's speech, a young bride, Rebecca M. Sandford, came forward to the altar and

Why Women Should Not Seek the Vote

Not every woman believed that giving political rights was an important goal. In 1869, Harriet Beecher Stowe, the author of Uncle Tom's Cabin, *and her sister, Catherine Beecher, argued instead that women should simply ask their fathers, husbands, and brothers for what they need rather than fight with them as politics necessarily requires.*

M any intelligent and benevolent persons imagine that the grand remedy for the heavy evils that oppress our sex is to introduce woman to political power and office, to make her a party in primary political meetings, in political caucuses, and in the scramble and fight for political offices; thus bringing into this dangerous *melée* the distinctive tempting power of her sex. Who can look at this new danger without dismay? . . .

Let us suppose that our friends have gained the ballot and the powers of office; are there any real beneficent measures for our sex, which they would enforce by law and penalties, that fathers, brothers, and husbands would not grant to a united petition of our sex, or even to a majority of the wise and good? Would these not confer what the wives, mothers, and sisters deemed best for themselves and the children they are to train, very much sooner than they would give power and office to our sex to enforce these advantages by law? Would it not be a wiser thing to *ask* for what we need, before trying so circuitous and dangerous a method? God has given to man the physical power, so that all that woman may gain, either by petitions or by ballot, will be the gift of love or of duty; and the ballot never will be accorded till benevolent and conscientious men are the majority—a millennial point far beyond our present ken.

Mary Beth Norton, ed., *Major Problems in American Women's History.* Lexington, MA: D.C. Heath and Company, 1989, p. 206.

asked the privilege of saying a few words. She said she was on her way westward, but hearing of this Convention, she had waited over one train to add her mite in favor of the demand now made by the true women of this day and generation. She eloquently advocated the just claims of woman to an entire equality with man. Her remarks were listened to with close attention, and produced a marked impression upon the audience, furnishing an evidence, if any were still needed, that Woman's voice and ability could effect much in the sacred desk (so-called), in legislative halls, or anywhere where true eloquence is required.

Her husband, who accompanied her, remained standing near her (with respectful silence) while she spoke as follows:

It is with diffidence that I speak upon the deliberations before us, not a diffidence resulting from any doubt of the worthiness of the cause, but from the fear that its *depth* and *power* can be but meagrely portrayed by me.

Woman's right—her civil right—equal with man's—not an equality of moral and religious influence, for who dare to deny her that? . . .

If you will galvanize her into civil liberty, you will find her capable of being in it, and of sustaining it. Place her in equal power, and you will find her capable of not abusing it! Give her the elective franchise, and there will be an unseen, yet a deep and universal movement of the people to elect into office only those who are pure in intention and honest in sentiment! Give her the privilege to co-operate in making the laws she submits to, and there will be harmony without severity, and justice without oppression. Make her, if married, a *living being* in the eye of the law—she will not assume beyond duty; give her right of property, and you may justly tax her patrimony as the result of her wages. Open to her your colleges—your legislative, your municipal, your domestic laws may be purified and ennobled. *Forbid her not*, and she will use moderation.

These thoughts of right and liberty are young with us. The American Independence was once young; and to what has it now progressed? The draft of *our* Declaration may, in some respects, be faulty and feeble. So may have been the first draft of the Constitution of the United States. But what right has it not protected, what grievance not redressed, and what exertions not encouraged? . . .

Here will be one effect, perhaps unlooked for, if we are raised to equal administration with man. It will classify intellect. The heterogeneous triflings which now, I am very sorry to say, occupy so much of our time, will be neglected; fashion's votaries will silently fall off; dishonest exertions for rank in society will be scorned; extravagance in toilet will be detested; that meagre and worthless pride of station will be forgotten; the honest earnings of dependents will be paid; popular demagogues crushed; imposters unpatronized; true genius sincerely encouraged; and, above all, pawned integrity redeemed. And why? Because enfranchised woman then will feel the burdens of her responsibilities, and can strive for elevation, and will reach all knowledge within her grasp.

If all this is accomplished, man need not fear pomposity, fickleness, or an unhealthy enthusiasm at his dear fireside; we can be as dutiful, submissive, endearing as daughters, wives and mothers, even if we hang the wreath of domestic harmony upon the eagle's talons. . . .

SARAH C. OWEN next read an address, earnestly portraying many of the wrongs and outrages to which woman is subjected, an extract of which follows: . . .

It is a generally received truth, that the proper study of mankind is *man;* virtually denying that *woman* is included in the intelligent part of creation; that she is endowed with mental powers that could be properly extended beyond the narrow bounds of the domestic circle. We have possessed our souls in all possible patience, waiting for some day-star of hope and promise to beam upon our pathway, assuring us that he who had robbed us would restore without this individual effort; but patience has expired, and hope fled; therefore we now raise the banner of equal rights, with the assurance that patience and perseverance is the secret of success in all crusades against oppression and wrong.

We hear the cry, "Who hath, or wherein have we robbed thee?" I assert that woman is robbed of all those inalienable rights which man enjoys, those which our Creator never thus unequally assigned to his children. And it needs no particular demonstration to prove that the disparity of intellect depends in no way on physical strength and stature; this idea has its origin in the bias of a wrong education, saying nothing of selfishness.

It has been reiterated from time immemorial that woman is the weaker vessel, that she was designed to occupy a lower sphere than man, to be subject to all the restraints he deems proper. . . .

In this christian land, in this day of intelligence, we are far behind those of heathen lands in centuries past, woman is considered of less value than the most abject slave. By law, five slaves in the scale of political power numbers the same as three white men, while one million of white women weigh just nothing at all. . . .

The Need for Action

Mrs. MOTT remarked that our aim should be to elevate the lowly and aid the weak. She compared the condition of woman to that of the free colored population, and dwelt upon the progress *they* had made within the last few years, urging woman to imitate them in their perseverance through oppression and prejudice, and said, "while woman is regarded as an inferior being, while the Bible is brought forward to prove the right of her present position, and while she is disposed to feel satisfied with it, all these efforts can do but little. We cannot expect to do much by meeting in Conventions for those borne down by the oppressor, unless the oppressed themselves *feel* and *act*, and while so little attention is paid to her education, and so little respect for woman.". . .

She said that she would grant that woman's intellect may be feeble, because she had been so long crushed; but is that any reason why she should be deprived of her equal rights? Does one man have fewer rights than another because his intellect is inferior? If not, why should woman? Let woman arise and demand her rights, and in a few years we shall see a different mental development. She regarded this as the beginning of the day when woman shall rise and occupy her appropriate position in society. . . .

The Seneca Falls Declaration of Sentiments

PRESIDENT in the Chair. A large and crowded audience still in attendance.

On motion, the Declaration of Sentiments was again read, and one hundred and seven signatures obtained, when another discussion ensued upon the dangerous doctrines. . . .

The following resolutions, which had been separately discussed, were again read. Amy Post moved their adoption by the meeting, which was carried with but two or three dissenting voices:

1. Resolved, That we petition our State Legislature for our right to the elective franchise, every year, until our prayer be granted.

2. Resolved, That it is an admitted principle of the American Republic, that the only just power of the Government is derived from the consent of the governed; and that taxation and representation are inseperable; and therefore, woman being taxed equally with man, ought not to be deprived of an equal representation in the government.

3. Resolved, That we deplore the apathy and indifference of woman in regard to her rights, thus restricting her to an inferior position in social, religious, and political life, and we urge her to claim an equal right to act on all subjects that interest the human family.

4. Resolved, That the assumption of law to settle estates of men who die without wills, having widows, is an insult to woman, and ought to be regarded as such by every lover of right and equality.

5. Whereas, The husband has the legal right to hire out his wife to service, collect her wages and appropriate it to his own exclusive and independent benefit; and, whereas, this has contributed to establish that hideous custom, the promise of obedience in the marriage contract, effectually,

though insidiously, reducing her almost to the condition of a *slave,* whatever freedom she may have in these respects, being granted as a privilege, not as a right, therefore,

Resolved, That we will seek the overthrow of this barbarous and unrighteous law; and conjure women no longer to promise obedience in the marriage covenant.

Resolved, That the universal doctrine of the inferiority of woman has ever caused her to distrust her own powers, and paralized her energies, and placed her in that degraded position from which the most strenuous and unremitting effort can alone redeem her. Only by faithful perseverance in the practical exercise of those talents, so long "wrapped in a napkin and buried under the earth," she will regain her long-lost equality with man.

Resolved, That in the persevering and independent course of Miss Blackwell, who recently attended a series of medical lectures in Geneva, and has now gone to Europe to graduate as a physician, we see a harbinger of the day when woman shall stand forth "redeemed and disenthralled," and perform those important duties which are so truly within her sphere.

Resolved, That those who believe the laboring classes of women are oppressed ought to do all in their power to raise their wages, beginning with their own household servants.

Resolved, That it is the duty of woman, whatever her complexion, to assume, as soon as possible, her true position of equality in the social circle, the church, and the state.

Resolved, That we tender our grateful acknowledgment to the Trustees of the Unitarian Church, who have kindly opened their doors for the use of this Convention.

Resolved, That we, the friends who are interested in this cause, gratefully accept the kind offer from the Trustees of the use of Protection Hall, to hold our meetings whenever we wish.

With hearts overflowing with grateful joy, the meeting adjourned *sine die.*

The Rationale for a Women's Suffrage Amendment

Elizabeth Cady Stanton

> Elizabeth Cady Stanton, a leading figure in the earliest stages
> of the women's rights movement, strongly believed that until
> women gained the right to vote, very little else in the way of
> women's rights could be achieved. In this address, delivered
> to the National Woman's Suffrage Convention in Washington,
> D.C., in 1869, Stanton forcefully argues that full political
> equality for women is so crucial that the Constitution must be
> changed to ensure that all women in America are given the
> right to vote. She links her demands for a woman's right to
> vote to the recently ratified Fifteenth Amendment, which
> granted former male slaves the right to vote. She suggests it is
> unfair that, while many ignorant men are given the right to
> vote, intelligent women are not given this same right. The
> elitism in this line of reasoning caused many supporters of
> women's rights to accept Stanton's conclusions while simul-
> taneously rejecting her rationale.

Those who represent what is called "the Woman's Rights
Movement," have argued their right to political equality from every standpoint of justice, religion, and logic, for
the last twenty years. They have quoted the Constitution, the
Declaration of Independence, the Bible, the opinions of
great men and women in all ages; they have plead the the-

Excerpted from *History of Woman Suffrage*, vol. 2, edited by Elizabeth Cady Stanton,
Susan B. Anthony, and Matilda Joslyn Gage (Rochester, NY: Charles Mann, 1889).

ory of our government; suffrage a natural, inalienable right; shown from the lessons of history, that one class can not legislate for another; that disfranchised classes must ever be neglected and degraded; and that all privileges are but mockery to the citizen, until he has a voice in the making and administering of law. Such arguments have been made over and over in conventions and before the legislatures of the several States. Judges, lawyers, priests, and politicians have said again and again, that our logic was unanswerable, and although much nonsense has emanated from the male tongue and pen on this subject, no man has yet made a fair argument on the other side. Knowing that we hold the Gibraltar rock of reason on this question, they resort to ridicule and petty objections. Compelled to follow our assailants, wherever they go, and fight them with their own weapons; when cornered with wit and sarcasm, some cry out, you have no logic on your platform, forgetting that we have no use for logic until they give us logicians at whom to hurl it, and if, for the pure love of it, we now and then rehearse the logic that is like a, b, c, to all of us, others cry out—the same old speeches we have heard these twenty years. It would be safe to say a hundred years, for they are the same our fathers used when battling old King George and the British Parliament for their right to representation, and a voice in the laws by which they were governed. There are no new arguments to be made on human rights, our work today is to apply to ourselves those so familiar to all; to teach man that woman is not an anomalous being, outside all laws and constitutions, but one whose rights are to be established by the same process of reason as that by which he demands his own.

When our [Founding] Fathers made out their famous bill of impeachment against England, they specified eighteen grievances. When the women of this country surveyed the situation in their first convention, they found they had precisely that number, and quite similar in character; and reading over the old revolutionary arguments of [Thomas] Jefferson, Patrick Henry, [James] Otis, and [John] Adams, they found they applied remarkably well to their case. The same arguments made in this country for extending suffrage from time to time, to white men, native born citizens, without property and education, and to foreigners; the same used by John Bright in England, to extend it to a million new voters, and the same used by the great Republican party to enfranchise a million black men in the South, all these arguments we have today to offer for woman, and one, in addition, stronger than all besides, the difference in man and woman. Because man and woman are the complement of one another, we need woman's thought in national affairs to make a safe and stable government.

The Republican party today congratulates itself on having carried the Fifteenth Amendment of the Constitution, thus securing "manhood suffrage" and establishing an aristocracy of sex on this continent. As several bills to secure Woman's Suffrage in the District and the Territories have been already presented in both houses of Congress, and . . . the question of so amending the Constitution as to extend suffrage to all the women of the country has been presented to the nation for consideration, it is not only the right but the duty of every thoughtful woman to express her opinion on a Sixteenth Amendment. While I hail the late discussions in Congress and the various bills presented as so many signs of progress, I am especially gratified with those . . . which forbid any State to deny the right of suffrage to any of its citizens on account of sex or color.

The Need for a Constitutional Amendment

This fundamental principle of our government—the equality of all the citizens of the republic—should be incorporated in the Federal Constitution, there to remain forever. To leave this question to the States and partial acts of Congress, is to defer indefinitely its settlement, for what is done by this Congress may be repealed by the next; and politics in the several States differ so widely, that no harmonious action on any question can ever be secured, except as a strict party measure. Hence, we appeal to the party now in power, everywhere, to end this protracted debate on suffrage, and declare it the inalienable right of every citizen who is amenable to the laws of the land, who pays taxes and the penalty of crime. We have a splendid theory of a genuine republic, why not realize it and make our government homogeneous, from Maine to California. . . .

I urge a speedy adoption of a Sixteenth Amendment for the following reasons:

A Threat to Liberty and Democracy

1. A government, based on the principle of caste and class, can not stand. The aristocratic idea, in any form, is opposed to the genius of our free institutions, to our own declaration of rights, and to the civilization of the age. All artificial distinctions, whether of family, blood, wealth, color, or sex, are equally oppressive to the subject classes, and equally destructive to national life and prosperity. Governments based on every form of aristocracy, on every degree and variety of inequality, have been tried in despotisms, monarchies, and republics, and all alike have perished. . . . Thus far, all nations have been built on caste and failed. Why, in this hour of reconstruction, with the experience of generations before us, make another experiment in the same direction? If serfdom, peasantry, and slavery have shattered kingdoms, deluged continents with blood, scattered republics like dust before the wind, and rent our own Union asunder, what kind of a government, think you, American statesmen, you can build, with the mothers of the race crouching at your feet, while iron-heeled peasants, serfs, and slaves, exalted by your hands, tread our inalienable rights into the dust? While all men, everywhere, are rejoicing in new-found liberties, shall woman alone be denied the rights, privileges, and immunities of citizenship? . . . While here, in our own land, slaves, but just rejoicing in the proclamation of emancipation, ignorant alike of its power and significance, have the ballot unasked, unsought, already laid at their feet—think you the daughters of [John] Adams, [Thomas] Jefferson, and Patrick Henry, in whose veins flows the blood of two Rev-

olutions, will forever linger round the camp-fires of an old barbarism, with no longings to join this grand army of freedom in its onward march to roll back the golden gates of a higher and better civilization? Of all kinds of aristocracy, that of sex is the most odious and unnatural; invading, as it does, our homes, desecrating our family altars, dividing those whom God has joined together, exalting the son above the mother who bore him, and subjugating, everywhere, moral power to brute force. Such a government would not be worth the blood and treasure so freely poured out in its long struggles for freedom. . . .

The Male Element Is Destructive

2. I urge a Sixteenth Amendment, because "manhood suffrage" or a man's government, is civil, religious, and social disorganization. The male element is a destructive force, stern, selfish, aggrandizing, loving war, violence, conquest, acquisition, breeding in the material and moral world alike discord, disorder, disease, and death. See what a record of blood and cruelty the pages of history reveal! Through what slavery, slaughter, and sacrifice, through what inquisitions and imprisonments, pains and persecutions, black codes and gloomy creeds, the soul of humanity has struggled for the centuries, while mercy has veiled her face and all hearts have been dead alike to love and hope! The male element has held high carnival [been completely dominant] thus far, it has fairly run riot from the beginning, overpowering the feminine element everywhere, crushing out all the diviner qualities in human nature, until we know but little of true manhood and womanhood, of the latter comparatively nothing, for it has scarce been recognized as a power until within the last century. Society is but the reflection of man himself, untempered by woman's thought, the hard iron rule we feel alike in the church, the state, and the home. No one need wonder at the disorganization, at the fragmentary condition of everything, when we remember that man, who represents but half a complete being, with but half an idea on every subject, has undertaken the absolute control of all sublunary matters.

People object to the demands of those whom they choose to call the strong-minded, because they say, "the right of suffrage will make the women masculine." That is just the difficulty in which we are involved today. Though disfranchised we have few women in the best sense; we have simply so many reflections, varieties, and dilutions of the masculine gender. The strong, natural characteristics of womanhood are repressed and ignored in dependence, for so long as man feeds woman she will try to please the giver and adapt herself to his condition. To keep a foothold in society woman must be as near like man as possible, reflect his ideas, opinions, virtues, motives, prejudices, and vices. She must respect his statutes, though they strip her of every inalienable right, and conflict with that higher law written by the finger of God on her own soul. She must believe his theology, though it pave the highways of hell with the skulls of new-born infants, and make God a monster of vengeance and hypocrisy. She must look at everything from its dollar and cent point of view, or she is a mere romancer. She must accept things as they are and make the best of them. To mourn over the miseries of others, the poverty of the poor, their hardships in jails, prisons, asylums, the horrors of war, cruelty, and brutality in every form, all this would be mere sentimentalizing. To protest against the intrigue, bribery, and corruption of public life, to desire that her sons might follow some business that did not involve lying, cheating, and a hard, grinding selfishness, would be arrant nonsense. In this way man has been moulding woman to his ideas by direct and positive influences, while she, if not a negation, has used indirect means to control him, and in most cases developed the very characteristics both in him and herself that needed repression. And now man himself stands appalled at the results of his own excesses, and mourns in bitterness that falsehood, selfishness and violence are the law of life. The need of this hour is not territory, gold mines, railroads, or specie payments, but a new evangel [positive proclamation] of womanhood, to exalt purity, virtue, morality, true religion, to lift man up into the higher realms of thought and action.

We ask woman's enfranchisement, as the first step toward the recognition of that essential element in government that can only secure the health, strength, and prosperity of the nation. Whatever is done to lift woman to her true position will help to usher in a new day of peace and perfection for the race. In speaking of the masculine element, I do not wish to be understood to say that all men are hard, selfish, and brutal, for many of the most beautiful spirits the world has known have been clothed with manhood; but I refer to those characteristics, though often marked in woman, that distinguish what is called the stronger sex. For example, the love of acquisition and conquest, the very pioneers of civilization, when expended on the earth, the sea, the elements, the riches and forces of Nature, are powers of destruction when used to subjugate one man to another or to sacrifice nations to ambition. Here that great conservator of woman's love, if permitted to assert itself, as it naturally would in freedom against oppression, violence, and war, would hold all these destructive forces in check, for woman knows the cost of life better than man does, and not with her consent would one drop of blood ever be shed, one life sacrificed in vain. . . . The present disorganization of society warns us, that in the dethronement of woman we have let loose the elements of violence and ruin that she only has the power to curb. If the civilization of the age calls for an extension of the suffrage, surely a government of the most virtuous, educated men and women would better represent the whole, and protect the interests of all than could the representation of either sex alone. But government gains no new element of strength in admitting all men to the ballot-box, for we have too much of the man-power there already. We see this in every department of legislation, and it is a common remark, that unless some new virtue is infused into our public life the nation is doomed to destruction. Will the foreign element, the dregs of China, Germany, England, Ireland, and Africa supply this needed force, or the nobler types of American womanhood who have taught our presidents, senators, and congressmen the rudiments of all they know?

Ignorant Men but Not Intelligent Women?

3. I urge a Sixteenth Amendment because, when "manhood suffrage" is established from Maine to California, woman has reached the lowest depths of political degradation. So long as there is a disfranchised class in this country, and that class its women, a man's government is worse than a white man's government with suffrage limited by property and educational qualifications, because in proportion as you multiply the rulers, the condition of the politically ostracised is more hopeless and degraded. John Stuart Mill, in his work on "Liberty," shows that the condition of one disfranchised man in a nation is worse than when the whole nation is under one man, because in the latter case, if the one man is despotic, the nation can easily throw him off, but what can one man do with a nation of tyrants over him? If American women find it hard to bear the oppressions of their own Saxon fathers, the best orders of manhood, what may they not be called to endure when all the lower orders of foreigners now crowding our shores legislate for them and their daughters. Think of Patrick and Sambo and Hans and Yung Tung, who do not know the difference between a monarchy and a republic, who can not read the Declaration of Independence or Webster's spelling-book, making laws for Lucretia Mott, Ernestine L. Rose, and Anna E. Dickinson. Think of jurors and jailors drawn from these ranks to watch and try young girls for the crime of infanticide, to decide the moral code by which the mothers of this Republic shall be governed? This manhood suffrage is an appalling question, and it would be well for thinking women, who seem to consider it so magnanimous to hold their own claims in abeyance until all men are crowned with citizenship, to remember that the most ignorant men are ever the most hostile to the equality of women, as they have known them only in slavery and degradation.

Go to our courts of justice, our jails and prisons; go into the world of work; into the trades and professions; into the temples of science and learning, and see what is meted out everywhere, to women—to those who have no advocates in our courts, no representatives in the councils of the nation. Shall we prolong and perpetuate such injustice, and by increasing this power risk worse oppressions for ourselves and daughters? It is an open, deliberate insult to American womanhood to be cast down under the iron-heeled peasantry of the Old World and the slaves of the New, as we shall be in the practical working of the Fifteenth Amendment, and the only atonement the Republican party can make is now to complete its work, by enfranchising the women of the nation. I have not forgotten their action four years ago, when Article XIV., Sec. 2, was amended by invidiously introducing the word "male" into the Federal Constitution, where it had never been before, thus counting out of the basis of representation all men not permitted to vote, thereby making it the interest of every State to enfranchise its male citizens, and virtually declaring it no crime to disfranchise its women. As political sagacity moved our rulers thus to guard the interests of the negro for party purposes, common justice might have compelled them to show like respect for their own mothers. . . .

Shall American statesmen, claiming to be liberal, so amend their constitutions as to make their wives and mothers the political inferiors of unlettered and unwashed ditch-diggers, boot-blacks, butchers, and barbers, fresh from the slave plantations of the South, and the effete civilizations of the Old World? While poets and philosophers, statesmen and men of science are all alike pointing to woman as the new hope for the redemption of the race, shall the freest Government on the earth be the first to establish an aristocracy based on sex alone? to exalt ignorance above education, vice above virtue, brutality and barbarism above refinement and religion? Not since God first called light out of darkness and order out of chaos, was there ever made so base a proposition as "manhood suffrage" in this American Republic, after all the discussions we have had on human rights in the last century. On all the blackest pages of history there is no record of an act like this, in any nation, where native born citizens, having the same religion, speaking the same language, equal to their rulers in wealth, family, and education, have been politically ostracised by their own countrymen, outlawed with savages, and subjected to the government of outside barbarians. Remember the Fifteenth Amendment takes in a larger population than the 2,000,000 black men on the Southern plantation. It takes in all the foreigners daily landing in our eastern cities, the Chinese crowding our western shores, the inhabitants of Alaska, and all those western isles that will soon be ours. American statesmen may flatter themselves that by superior intelligence and political sagacity the higher orders of men will always govern, but when the ignorant foreign vote already holds the balance of power in all the large cities by sheer force of numbers, it is simply a question of impulse or passion, bribery or fraud, how our elections will be carried. When the highest offices in the gift of the people are bought and sold in Wall Street, it is a mere chance who will be our rulers. Whither is a nation tending when brains count for less than bullion, and clowns make laws for queens? . . . In our Southern States even, before the war, women were not degraded below the working population. They were not humiliated in seeing their coachmen, gardeners, and waiters go to the polls to legislate for them, but here, in this boasted Northern civilization, women of wealth and education, who pay taxes and obey the laws, who in morals and intellect are the peers of their proudest rulers, are thrust outside the pale of political consideration with minors, paupers, lunatics, traitors, idiots, with those guilty of bribery, larceny, and infamous crimes.

Would those gentlemen who are on all sides telling the women of the nation not to press their claims until the negro is safe beyond peradventure, be willing themselves to stand aside and trust all their interests to hands like these? The educated women of this nation feel as much interest in republican institutions, the preservation of the country, the good of the race, their own elevation and success, as any man possibly can, and we have the same distrust in man's power to legislate for us, that he has in woman's power to legislate wisely for herself.

Remembering Sojourner Truth's "Ain't I a Woman?" Speech

Frances D. Gage

Frances D. Gage, an opponent of slavery and a proponent of women's suffrage, describes the occasion when Sojourner Truth, perhaps the most famous African American woman to speak out for women's suffrage, addressed a women's rights convention in Akron, Ohio, in 1851. Unlike many of her fellow speakers, who seemed unable to respond to the numerous male hecklers in the audience, Sojourner Truth forcefully rebutted a minister's claim that women were too weak and fragile to vote. Sojourner Truth was a fifty-four-year-old, imposing former slave who, during her speech, rolled up her sleeves to show the audience her muscles while asking the famous question, "Ain't I a woman?"

The leaders of the movement trembled on seeing a tall, gaunt black woman in a gray dress and white turban, surmounted with an uncouth sun bonnet, march deliberately into the church, walk with the air of a queen up the aisle, and take her seat upon the pulpit steps. A buzz of disapprobation was heard all over the house, and there fell on the listening ear, "An abolition affair!" "Woman's rights and niggers!" "I told you so!" "Go it, darkey!"

Excerpted from *History of Woman Suffrage*, vol. 1, edited by Elizabeth Cady Stanton, Susan B. Anthony, and Matilda Joslyn Gage (Rochester, NY: Charles Mann, 1889).

I chanced on that occasion to wear my first laurels in public life as president of the meeting. At my request order was restored, and the business of the Convention went on. Morning, afternoon, and evening exercises came and went. Through all these sessions old Sojourner, quiet and reticent as the "Lybian Statue," sat crouched against the wall on the corner of the pulpit stairs, her sun bonnet shading her eyes, her elbows on her knees, her chin resting upon her broad, hard palms. At intermission she was busy selling the "Life of Sojourner Truth," a narrative of her own strange and adventurous life. Again and again, timorous and trembling ones came to me and said, with earnestness, "Don't let her speak, Mrs. Gage, it will ruin us. Every newspaper in the land will have our cause mixed up with abolition and niggers, and we shall be utterly denounced." My only answer was, "We shall see when the time comes."

Male Objections

The second day the work waxed warm. Methodist, Baptist, Episcopal, Presbyterian, and Universalist ministers came in to hear and discuss the resolutions presented. One claimed superior rights and privileges for man, on the ground of "superior intellect"; another, because of the "manhood of Christ; if God had desired equality of woman, He would have given some token of His will through the birth, life, and death of the Savior." Another gave us a theological view of the "sin of our first mother."

There were very few women in those days who dared to "speak in meeting"; and the august teachers of the people were seemingly getting the better of us, while the boys in the galleries, and the sneerers among the pews, were hugely enjoying the discomfiture, as they supposed, of the "strongminded." Some of the tender-skinned friends were on the point of losing dignity, and the atmosphere betokened a storm. When slowly from her seat in the corner rose Sojourner Truth, who, till now, had scarcely lifted her head. "Don't let her speak!" gasped half a dozen in my ear. She moved slowly and solemnly to the front, laid her old bonnet at her feet, and turned her great speaking eyes to me. There was a hissing sound of disapprobation above and below. I rose and announced "Sojourner Truth," and begged the audience to keep silence for a few moments.

Sojourner Speaks

The tumult subsided at once, and every eye was fixed on this almost Amazon form, which stood nearly six feet high, head erect, and eyes piercing the upper air like one in a dream. At her first word there was a profound hush. She spoke in deep tones, which, though not loud, reached every ear in the house, and away through the throng at the doors and windows.

"Wall, chilern, whar dar is so much racket dar must be somethin' out o' kilter. I tink dat 'twixt de niggers of de Souf and de womin at de Norf, all talkin' 'bout rights, de white men will be in a fix pretty soon. But what's all dis here talkin' 'bout?

"Dat man ober dar say dat womin needs to be helped into carriages, and lifted ober ditches, and to hab de best place everywhar. Nobody eber helps me into carriages, or ober mud-puddles, or gibs me any best place!" And raising herself to her full height, and her voice to a pitch like rolling thunder, she asked, "And ain't I a woman? Look at me! Look at my arm! (and she bared her right arm to the shoulder, showing her tremendous muscular power). I have ploughed, and planted, and gathered into barns, and no man could head me! And ain't I a woman? I could work as much and eat as much as a man—when I could get it—and bear de lash as well! And ain't I a woman? I have borne thirteen chilern, and seen 'em mos' all sold off to slavery, and when I cried out with my mother's grief, none but Jesus heard me! And ain't I a woman?

"Den dey talks 'bout dis ting in de head; what dis dey call it?" ("Intellect," whispered some one near.) "Dat's it, honey. What's dat got to do wid womin's rights or nigger's rights? If my cup won't hold but a pint, and yourn holds a quart, wouldn't ye be mean not to let me have my little half-measure full?" And she pointed her significant finger, and

sent a keen glance at the minister who had made the argument. The cheering was long and loud.

"Den dat little man in black dar, he say women can't have
as much rights as men, 'cause Christ wan't a woman! Whar
did your Christ come from?" Rolling thunder couldn't have
stilled that crowd, as did those deep, wonderful tones, as she
stood there with outstretched arms and eyes of fire. Raising
her voice still louder, she repeated, "Whar did your Christ
come from? From God and a woman! Man had nothin' to
do wid Him." Oh, what a rebuke that was to that little man.

Turning again to another objector, she took up the defense
of Mother Eve. I can not follow her through it all. It was
pointed, and witty, and solemn, eliciting at almost every sentence deafening applause; and she ended by asserting: "If
de fust woman God ever made was strong enough to turn de
world upside down all alone, dese women togedder (and she
glanced her eye over the platform) ought to be able to turn
it back, and get it right side up again! And now dey is asking to do it, de men better let 'em." Long-continued cheering greeted this. "'Bleeged to ye for hearin' on me, and now
ole Sojourner han't got nothin' more to say."

The Tide Turns

Amid roars of applause, she returned to her corner, leaving
more than one of us with streaming eyes, and hearts beating
with gratitude. She had taken us up in her strong arms and
carried us safely over the slough of difficulty turning the
whole tide in our favor. I have never in my life seen anything
like the magical influence that subdued the mobbish spirit of
the day, and turned the sneers and jeers of an excited crowd
into notes of respect and admiration. Hundreds rushed up to
shake hands with her, and congratulate the glorious old
mother, and bid her God-speed on her mission of "testifyin'
agin concerning the wickedness of this 'ere people."

Praise for
A Religion of One's Own

"Moore has marshaled all the wisdom and imaginative insights he has accrued over the years and put them together in a sumptuous and soul-stirring description of an openhearted and flexible path for all of us—young and old, religious and spiritually independent. Here at last is a substantive book that respects the riches of religion, spirituality, and secularity and equips the saints (that would be us) to embrace all the wild possibilities as we head out into the new territories ahead." —*Spirituality & Practice*

"When [Moore] is read closely, his depth is apparent. . . . He stands to make some new converts to the noninstitutional ranks of spirituality." —*Publishers Weekly*

"[Moore] offers a new vision of how seekers can fashion their own connection to the sacred out of the materials of ancient faiths and everyday life." —*Psychology Today*

"[Moore's] counsel is consistently sensible and affirming. This book should appeal to many of the unchurched, as well as the faithful across traditions." —*Library Journal*

"Guided by Taoism, Christianity, Greek mythology, Buddhism, Sufism, transcendentalism, and Native American belief . . . [*A Religion of One's Own*] wears its spirit of tolerance on its sleeve." —*Kirkus Reviews*

Can Women Win the Right to Vote If They Wear Dresses?

Gerrit Smith, Elizabeth Cady Stanton, and Frances D. Gage

Gerrit Smith, fundamentally a supporter of the goals of the women's rights movement, writes a letter to his cousin and prominent leader of the movement, Elizabeth Cady Stanton. In his letter, he argues that the true obstacle to fundamental rights for women is not the right to vote. Instead he suggests that women must do away with the symbols of their femininity, such as their dresses. If women abandon these imprisoning symbols that men associate with traditional notions of female weakness and fragility, then perhaps they would be taken seriously as individuals deserving of equal rights. Until they do this, their outward trappings will undermine their arguments for political independence. Elizabeth Cady Stanton replies to her cousin by suggesting that his despair over the failures of the women's rights movement reflects his disappointment over the lack of concrete gains in the antislavery, pro-temperance, and pro-suffrage movements.

Smith's letter was printed in a newspaper run by the famous antislavery advocate Frederick Douglass. When the issue was run, Frances D. Gage, another prominent suffragist, felt that she too must respond to Smith's arguments. Writing her own editorial to Douglass, Gage takes Smith's words literally, pointing out the ridiculousness of asserting that the righteous demand for political rights is in any way compromised by a woman's attire.

Excerpted from *History of Woman Suffrage*, vol. 1, edited by Elizabeth Cady Stanton, Susan B. Anthony, and Matilda Joslyn Gage (Rochester, NY: Charles Mann, 1889).

PETERBORO, *December* 1, 1855.

E LIZABETH C. STANTON.—*My Dear Friend:*—The "Woman's Rights Movement" has deeply interested your generous heart, and you have ever been ready to serve it with your vigorous understanding. It is, therefore, at the risk of appearing somewhat unkind and uncivil, that I give my honest answer to your question. You would know why I have so little faith in this movement. I reply, that it is not in the proper hands; and that the proper hands are not yet to be found. The present age, although in advance of any former age, is, nevertheless, very far from being sufficiently under the sway of reason to take up the cause of woman, and carry it forward to success. . . .

The object of the "Woman's Rights Movement" is nothing less than to recover the rights of woman—nothing less than to achieve her independence. She is now the dependent of man; and, instead of rights, she has but privileges—the mere concessions (always revocable and always uncertain) of the other sex to her sex. I say nothing against this object. It is as proper as it is great; and until it is realized, woman can not be half herself, nor can man be half himself. I rejoice in this object; and my sorrow is, that they, who are intent upon it, are not capable of adjusting themselves to it—not high-souled enough to consent to those changes and sacrifices in themselves, in their positions and relations, essential to the attainment of this vital object. . . .

Women's Clothing as a Barrier to Woman's Rights

Voluntarily wearing, in common with their sex, a dress which imprisons and cripples them, they, nevertheless, follow up this absurdity with the greater one of coveting and demanding a social position no less full of admitted rights, and a relation to the other sex no less full of independence, than such position and relation would naturally and necessarily have been, had they scorned a dress which leaves them less than half their personal power of self-subsistence and usefulness. I admit that the mass of women are not chargeable with this

latter absurdity of cherishing aspirations and urging claims
so wholly and so glaringly at war with this voluntary imprisonment and this self-degradation. They are content in their
helplessness and poverty and destitution of rights. Nay, they
are so deeply deluded as to believe that all this belongs to
their natural and unavoidable lot. But the handful of women
of whom I am here complaining—the woman's rights
women—persevere just as blindly and stubbornly as do other
women, in wearing a dress that both marks and makes their
impotence, and yet, O amazing inconsistency! they are
ashamed of their dependence, and remonstrate against its injustice. They claim that the fullest measure of rights and independence and dignity shall be accorded to them, and yet
they refuse to place themselves in circumstances corre-
sponding with their claim. . . .

I admit that the dress of woman is not the primal cause of
her helplessness and degradation. That cause is to be found
in the false doctrines and sentiments of which the dress is
the outgrowth and symbol. On the other hand, however,
these doctrines and sentiments would never have become
the huge bundle they now are, and they would probably have
all languished, and perhaps all expired, but for the dress.
For, as in many other instances, so in this, and emphatically
so in this, the cause is made more efficient by the reflex influence of the effect. Let woman give up the irrational
modes of clothing her person, and these doctrines and sentiments would be deprived of their most vital aliment by being deprived of their most natural expression. . . .

Were woman to throw off the dress, which, in the eye of
chivalry and gallantry, is so well adapted to womanly grace-
fulness and womanly helplessness, and to put on a dress that
would leave her free to work her own way through the world,
I see not but that chivalry and gallantry would nearly or quite
die out. No longer would she present herself to man, now in
the bewitching character of a plaything, a doll, an idol, and
now in the degraded character of his servant. But he would
confess her transmutation into his equal; and, therefore, all
occasion for the display of chivalry and gallantry toward her

Surrounded by curious onlookers, a woman campaigns for the right to vote.

on the one hand, and tyranny on the other, would have passed away. Only let woman attire her person fitly for the whole battle of life—that great and often rough battle, which she is as much bound to fight as man is, and the common sense expressed in the change will put to flight all the nonsensical fancies about her superiority to man, and all the nonsensical fancies about her inferiority to him. No more will then be heard of her being made of a finer material than man is made of; and, on the contrary, no more will then be heard of her being but the complement of man, and of its taking both a man and a woman (the woman, of course, but a small part of it) to make up a unit. . . .

Failing to See the Connection

I am amazed that the intelligent women engaged in the "Woman's Rights Movement," see not the relation between their dress and the oppressive evils which they are striving to throw off. I am amazed that they do not see that their dress is indispensable to keep in countenance the policy and purposes out of which those evils grow.

Women are holding their meetings; and with great ability do they urge their claim to the rights of property and suffrage. But, as in the case of the colored man, the great needed change is in himself, so, also, in the case of woman, the great needed change is in herself. Of what comparative avail would be her exercise of the right of suffrage, if she is still to remain the victim of her present false notions of herself and of her relations to the other sex?—false notions so emphatically represented and perpetuated by her dress? Moreover, to concede to her the rights of property would be to benefit her comparatively little, unless she shall resolve to break out from her clothes-prison, and to undertake right earnestly, as right earnestly as a man, to get property. . . .

Righteous Demands but Little Action

The next "Woman's Rights Convention" will, I take it for granted, differ but little from its predecessors. It will abound in righteous demands and noble sentiments, but not in the evidence that they who enunciate these demands and sentiments are prepared to put themselves in harmony with what they conceive and demand. In a word, for the lack of such preparation and of the deep earnestness, which alone can prompt to such preparation, it will be, as has been every other Woman's Rights Convention, a failure. Could I see it made up of women whose dress would indicate their translation from cowardice to courage; from slavery to freedom; from the kingdom of fancy and fashion and foolery to the kingdom of reason and righteousness, then would I hope for the elevation of woman, aye, and of man too, as perhaps I have never yet hoped. . . .

Woman must first fight against herself—against personal

and mental habits so deep-rooted and controlling, and so seemingly inseparable from herself, as to be mistaken for her very nature. And when she has succeeded there, an easy victory will follow. But where shall be the battle-ground for this indispensable self-conquest? She will laugh at my answer when I tell her, that her dress, aye, her dress, must be that battle-ground. What! no wider, no sublimer field than this to reap her glories in! My further answer is, that if she shall reap them anywhere, she must first reap them there. I add, that her triumph there will be her triumph everywhere; and that her failure there will be her failure everywhere.

Affectionately yours,

GERRIT SMITH.

• • •

SENECA FALLS, *Dec.* 21, 1855.
MY DEAR COUSIN:—Your letter on the "Woman's Right Movement" I have thoroughly read and considered. I thank you, in the name of woman, for having said what you have on so many vital points. You have spoken well for a man whose convictions on this subject are the result of reason and observation; but they alone whose souls are fired through personal experience and suffering can set forth the height and depth, the source and center of the degradation of women; they alone can feel a steadfast faith in their own native energy and power to accomplish a final triumph over all adverse surroundings, a speedy and complete success. You say you have but little faith in this reform, because the changes we propose are so great, so radical, so comprehensive; whilst they who have commenced the work are so puny, feeble, and undeveloped. The mass of women are developed at least to the point of discontent, and that, in the dawn of this nation, was considered a most dangerous point in the British Parliament, and is now deemed equally so on a Southern plantation. In the human soul, the steps between discontent and action are few and short indeed. You, who suppose the mass of women contented, know but little of the silent indignation, the deep and settled disgust with which they contemplate our present social arrangements. . . .

The Profound Need for Equality

We who have spoken out, have declared our rights, political and civil; but the entire revolution about to dawn upon us by the acknowledgment of woman's social equality, has been seen and felt but by the few. The rights, to vote, to hold property, to speak in public, are all-important; but there are great social rights, before which all others sink into utter insignificance. The cause of woman is, as you admit, a broader and a deeper one than any with which you compare it; and this, to me, is the very reason why it must succeed. It is not a question of meats and drinks, of money and lands, but of human rights—the sacred right of a woman to her own person, to all her God-given powers of body and soul. Did it ever enter into the mind of man that woman too had an inalienable right to life, liberty, and the pursuit of her individual happiness? Did he ever take in the idea that to the mother of the race, and to her alone, belonged the right to say when a new being should be brought into the world? Has he, in the gratification of his blind passions, ever paused to think whether it was with joy and gladness that she gave up ten or twenty years of the heyday of her existence to all the cares and sufferings of excessive maternity? Our present laws, our religious teachings, our social customs on the whole question of marriage and divorce, are most degrading to woman. . . . A true marriage relation has far more to do with the elevation of woman than the style and cut of her dress. Dress is a matter of taste, of fashion; it is changeable, transient, and may be doffed or donned at the will of the individual; but institutions, supported by laws, can be overturned but by revolution. We have no reason to hope that pantaloons would do more for us than they have done for man himself. The negro slave enjoys the most unlimited freedom in his attire, not surpassed even by the fashions of Eden in its palmiest days; yet in spite of his dress, and his manhood, too, he is a slave still. Was the old Roman in his toga less of a man than he now is in swallow-tail and tights? Did the flowing robes of Christ Himself render His life less grand and beautiful? In regard to dress, where you claim to be so radical, you are far from consistent. . . .

A Letter Written Out of Despair

Your letter, my noble cousin, must have been written in a most desponding mood, as all the great reforms of the day seem to you on the verge of failure. . . . When you compare the public sentiment and social customs of our day with what they were fifty years ago, how can you despair of the temperance cause? With a Maine Law and divorce for drunkenness, the rum-seller and drunkard must soon come to terms. Let woman's motto be, "No union with Drunkards," and she will soon bring this long and well-fought battle to a triumphant close.

Neither should you despair of the anti-slavery cause; with its martyrs, its runaway slaves, its legal decisions in almost every paper you take up, the topic of debate in our national councils, our political meetings, and our literature, it seems as if the nation were all alive on this question. True, four millions of slaves groan in their chains still, but every man in this nation has a higher idea of individual rights than he had twenty years ago.

As to the cause of woman, I see no signs of failure. We already have a property law, which in its legitimate effects must elevate the *femme covert* [married woman] into a living, breathing woman, a wife into a property-holder, who can make contracts, buy and sell. In a few years we shall see how well it works. It needs but little forethought to perceive that in due time these large property-holders must be represented in the Government; and when the mass of women see that there is some hope of becoming voters and law-makers, they will take to their rights as naturally as the negro to his heels when he is sure of success. . . . If you truly believe that man is woman, and woman is man; if you believe that all the burning indignation that fires your soul at the sight of injustice and oppression, if suffered in your own person, would nerve you to a life-long struggle for liberty and independence, then know that what you feel, I feel too, and what I feel the mass of women feel also. . . . Talk not to us of chivalry, that died long ago. Where do you see it? No gallant knight presents himself at the bar of justice to pay the penalty of our crimes. We suffer in our own persons, on the gallows, and in prison walls. . . . There is no display of gallantry in your written codes. In social life, true, a man in love will jump to pick up a glove or bouquet for a silly girl of sixteen, whilst at home he will permit his aged mother to carry pails of water and armfuls of wood, or his wife to lug a twenty-pound baby, hour after hour, without ever offering to relieve her. I have seen a great many men priding themselves on their good breeding—gentlemen, born and educated—who never manifest one iota of spontaneous gallantry toward the women of their own household. . . .

If a short dress is to make the men less gallant than they now are, I beg the women at our next convention to add at least two yards more to every skirt they wear. . . .

Affectionately yours,
ELIZABETH CADY STANTON.

• • •

FREDERICK DOUGLASS.—*Dear Sir:*—In your issue of Dec. 1st, I find a letter from Hon. Gerrit Smith to Elizabeth C. Stanton, in reference to the Woman's Rights Movement, showing cause, through labored columns, why it has proved a failure.

This article, though addressed to Mrs. Stanton, is an attack upon every one engaged in the cause. For he boldly asserts that the movement "is not in proper hands, and that the proper hands are not yet to be found." I will not deny the assertion, but must still claim the privilege of working in a movement that involves not only my own interest, but the interests of my sex, and through us the interests of a whole humanity. And though I may be but a John the Baptist, unworthy to unloose the latchet of the shoes of those who are to come in *short skirts* to redeem the world, I still prefer that humble position to being Peter to deny my Master, or a Gerrit Smith to assert that truth *can* fail.

I do not propose to enter into a full criticism of Mr. Smith's long letter. He has made the whole battle-ground of the Woman's Rights Movement her dress. Nothing brighter, nothing nobler than a few inches of calico or brocade added to or taken from her skirts, is to decide this great and glorious question—to give her freedom or to continue her a slave. This argument, had it come from one of less influence than Gerrit Smith, would have been simply ridiculous. But coming from *him*, the almost oracle of a large portion of our reformers, it becomes worthy of an answer from every earnest woman in our cause. I will not say one word in defense of our present mode of dress. Not I; but bad as it is, and cumbersome and annoying, I still feel that we can wear it, and yet be lovers of liberty, speaking out our deep feeling, portraying our accumulated wrongs, saving ourselves for a time yet from that antagonism which we must inevitably meet when we don the semi-male attire. We *must own ourselves under the law first*, own our bodies, our earnings, our genius, and our consciences; then we will turn to the lesser matter of what shall be the garniture of the body. Was the old Roman less a man in his cumbrous toga, than Washington in his tights? Was Christ less a Christ in His vesture, woven without a seam, than He would have been in the suit of a Broadway dandy?

Truth Does Not Depend on Dress

"Moreover, to concede to her rights of property, would be to benefit her comparatively little, unless she shall resolve to break out of her clothes-prison, and to undertake right earnestly, as earnestly as a man, to get property." So says Gerrit Smith. And he imputes the want of earnestness to her clothes. It is a new doctrine that high and holy purposes go from without inward, that the garments of men or women govern and control their aspirations. But do not women *now* work right earnestly? Do not the German women and our market women labor right earnestly? Do not the wives of our farmers and mechanics toil? Is not the work of the *mothers* in our land as important as that of the father? "Labor is the foundation of wealth." The reason that our women are "paupers," is not that they do not labor "right earnestly," but that the law gives their earnings into the hands of manhood. Mr. Smith says, "That women are helpless, is no wonder, so long as they are paupers"; he might add, no wonder that the slaves of the cotton plantation are helpless, so long as they are paupers. What reduces both the woman and the slave to this condition? The law which gives the husband and the master entire control of the person and earnings of each; the law that robs each of the rights and liberties that every "free white male citizen" takes to himself as God-given. Truth falling from the lips of a Lucretia Mott in long skirts is none the less truth, than if uttered by a Lucy Stone in short dress, or a Helen Maria Weber in pants and swallow-tail coat. And I can not yet think so meanly of manly justice, as to believe it will yield simply to a change of garments. Let us assert our right to be free. Let us get out of our prison-house of law. Let us own ourselves, our earnings, our genius; let us have power to control as well as to earn and to own; then will each woman adjust her dress to her relations in life. . . .

ROCHESTER, *Dec.* 24, 1855. FRANCES D. GAGE

Chapter 2

Making a Case for National Women's Suffrage

Chapter Preface

The addition of the Fifteenth Amendment to the United States Constitution in 1870 brought to the attention of some members of the women's suffrage movement that the goal of universal female suffrage could only be achieved with a national solution—most likely, a separate constitutional amendment for women's voting rights. Until that point, most advocates of women's suffrage believed that change would come about by convincing each state to modify its laws. But the Fifteenth Amendment stated that "The right of citizens of the United States to vote shall not be denied or abridged by the United States or by any state on account of race, color, or previous condition of servitude." Although the wording implied that *male* suffrage was the only right that the national government was pursuing, the phrasing also demonstrated that a constitutional amendment could instantaneously change both federal and state laws.

This is not to say that supporters of women's suffrage were willing to reject other potential national remedies. One approach was simply for women to assert that they already had the right to vote given the fact that the Constitution makes no formal distinctions between male and female citizens. However, this approach was short-lived. The Supreme Court explicitly and unanimously rejected the notion that women already had the right to vote in the famous court case *Minor v. Happesett* in 1875.

Another avenue to gain women's suffrage was to win voting rights in the new states and territories that were being admitted to the Union during the period of westward expansion. Since each new territory or state had to submit to Congress its proposed system of government (including details about the method of electing public officials), those territories or states that proposed female suffrage could spark a debate on this issue in the U.S. Congress. These debates would prove useful because they would alert supporters of women's suffrage about the perceived merits of and opposition to granting women the right to vote. Furthermore, since approval from the House and the Senate would most likely be needed to pass any constitutional amendment, these congressional debates would give suffragists useful information about which ideas they needed to provide to convince skeptics of the righteousness of female suffrage.

The Constitution Grants Women's Suffrage

Victoria Claflin Woodhull

> Victoria Claflin Woodhull was the first woman to run for
> president in 1872, as a candidate for the Equal Rights Party.
> One year before her unsuccessful bid for the White House,
> Woodhull argued that women had always had the right to vote
> since 1789, when the U.S. Constitution became the supreme
> law of the land. Her 1871 *A Lecture on Constitutional Equal-
> ity* presents the argument that women are granted the right to
> vote by the wording of the Constitution. For example, she
> suggests that, since the Constitution refers to "persons" rather
> than "men" and "women," this implies the intention of the
> Founding Fathers to grant women the right to vote. Therefore,
> she concludes that women should simply go to the polls at the
> next election and exercise their rights by voting for their pre-
> ferred candidates. Unfortunately, the courts, including the
> Supreme Court, never accepted Woodhull's line of reasoning,
> leaving the suffrage movement to continue its fight for female
> enfranchisement.

I now do proclaim, to the women of the United States of
America, that they are enfranchised. That they are, by
the Constitution of the Union, by the recognition of its Congress, by the action of a state, by the exercise of its func-
tions, henceforth entitled in all the states of the Union, and

Excerpted from *A Lecture on Constitutional Equality*, by Victoria Claflin Woodhull (New
York: Journeyman Printed Cooperative Association, 1871).

in all its territories, *to free and equal suffrage with men.*

This has been established by Wyoming. In the elections therein held women voted. . . .

From this exercise of female suffrage in Wyoming comes the legal, the undeniable fact, that each state has now imposed upon it the necessity, *not of granting* the right of suffrage to woman, for it exists, but of denying it if it is to be restrained—but how! Not by a legislative act, that is not sufficient, but by a convention, with its act to be approved by a vote of the *people* of whom the women would be voters also! Until a denial is accomplished in this manner woman has now, and will retain, *the right of suffrage in every state and territory of this Union.* . . .

Constitutional Evidence

That the framers of the Constitution had woman's rights clearly in their minds is borne out by its whole structure. Nowhere is the word *man* used in contradistinction to *woman.* They avoided both terms and used the word "persons" for the same reason as they avoided the word "slavery," namely, to prevent an untimely contest over rights which might prematurely be discussed to the injury of the infant republic. . . .

The issue upon the question of female suffrage being thus definitely settled, and its rights inalienably secured to woman, a brighter future dawns upon the country. Woman can now unite in purifying the elements of political strife— in restoring the government to pristine integrity, strength and vigor. To do this, many reforms become of absolute necessity. Prominent in these are:

A complete reform in the congressional and legislative work, by which all political discussion shall be banished from legislative halls, and debate be limited to the actual business of the people.

A complete reform in executive and departmental conduct, by which the president and the secretaries of the United States, and the governors and state officers, shall be forced to recognize that they are the servants of the people, appointed to attend to the business of the people, and not for the purpose of perpetuating their official positions, or of securing the plunder of public trusts for the enrichment of their political adherents and supporters.

A reform in the tenure of office, by which the presidency shall be limited to one term, with a retiring life pension, and

Victoria Claflin Woodhull

a permanent seat in the federal Senate, where his presidential experience may become serviceable to the nation, and on the dignity and life emolument of Presidential Senator he shall be placed above all other political positions, and be excluded from all professional pursuits. . . .

A reform between the relations of the employer and employed, by which shall be secured the practice of the great natural law, of one-third of time to labor, one-third to recreation and one-third to rest, that by this intellectual improvement and physical development may go on to that perfection which the Almighty Creator designed. . . .

A reform in the system of crime punishment, by which the death penalty shall no longer be inflicted—by which the hardened criminal shall have no human chance of being let loose to harass society until the term of the sentence, whatever that may be, shall have expired, and by which, during that term, the entire prison employment shall be for—and the product thereof be faithfully paid over to—the support of the criminal's family, instead of being absorbed by the legal thieves to whom, in most cases, the administration of prison discipline has been intrusted, and by whom atrocities are perpetrated in the secrecy of the prison inclosure, which, were they revealed, would shock the moral sense of all mankind.

In the broadest sense, I claim to be the friend of equal rights, a faithful worker in the cause of human advancement; and more especially the friend, supporter, co-laborer with those who strive to encourage the poor and the friendless. . . .

If I obtain . . . the position of President of the United States, I promise that woman's strength and woman's will, with God's support, if he vouchsafe it, shall open to them, and to this country, a new career of greatness in the race of nations. . . . In accordance with the above, we shall assume the new position that the rights of women under the Constitution are complete, and here-after we shall contend, not for a Sixteenth Amendment to the Constitution, but that the Constitution already recognizes women as citizens, and that they are justly entitled to all the privileges and immunities of citizens.

It will therefore be our duty to call on women everywhere to come boldly forward and exercise the right they are thus guaranteed. It is not to be expected that men who assume that they alone, as citizens of the United States, are entitled to all the immunities and privileges guaranteed by the Constitution, will consent that women may exercise the right of suffrage until they are compelled. . . . We will never cease the struggle until they are recognized, and we see women established in their true position of equality with the *rest of the citizens* of the United States.

The Fourteenth Amendment Grants Women's Suffrage

Susan B. Anthony

In 1872, Susan B. Anthony, a cofounder of the National
Woman Suffrage Association, and sixteen other women registered to vote in the presidential election. They argued that the
Fourteenth Amendment to the Constitution made all U.S.-
born Americans—men and women alike—citizens. Since voting is an important citizenship right, Anthony believed that
the Fourteenth Amendment automatically granted women the
right to vote. While all seventeen women were arrested after
casting their ballots, only Anthony was actually taken to trial,
indicating her importance in the women's suffrage movement.

Leading up to her trial, which was held in June 1873,
Anthony delivered versions of this speech throughout New
York to proclaim her innocence and to champion the cause of
women's suffrage. The judge in her trial ordered the jury to
find Anthony guilty, without allowing her to testify on her own
behalf. She was fined $100, yet she refused to pay. No further
action was taken against Susan B. Anthony for this incident.

Friends and Fellow-Citizens:—I stand before you under
indictment for the alleged crime of having voted at the
last presidential election, without having a lawful right to
vote. It shall be my work this evening to prove to you that
in thus doing, I not only committed no crime, but instead

Excerpted from *The Life and Work of Susan B. Anthony*, vol. 2, edited by Isa Husted
Harper (Indianapolis, IN: The Bowen-Merrill Company, 1898).

simply exercised my citizen's right, guaranteed to me and all United States citizens by the National Constitution beyond the power of any State to deny. . . .

The Declaration of Independence, the United States Constitution, the constitutions of the several states and the organic laws of the territories, all alike propose to *protect* the people in the exercise of their God-given rights. Not one of them pretends to bestow rights.

> All men are created equal, and endowed by their Creator with certain inalienable rights. Among these are life, liberty and the pursuit of happiness. To secure these, governments are instituted among men, deriving their just powers from the consent of the governed.

Here is no shadow of government authority over rights, or exclusion of any class from their full and equal enjoyment. Here is pronounced the right of all men, and "consequently," as the Quaker preacher said, "of all women," to a voice in the government. And here, in this first paragraph of the Declaration, is the assertion of the natural right of all to the ballot; for how can "the consent of the governed" be given, if the right to vote be denied? Again:

> Whenever any form of government becomes destructive of these ends, it is the right of the people to alter or abolish it, and to institute a new government, laying its foundations on such principles, and organizing its powers in such form, as to them shall seem most likely to effect their safety and happiness.

Surely the right of the whole people to vote is here clearly implied; for however destructive to their happiness this government might become, a disfranchised class could neither alter nor abolish it, nor institute a new one, except by the old brute force method of insurrection and rebellion. One-half of the people of this nation today are utterly powerless to blot from the statute books an unjust law, or to write there a new and a just one. The women, dissatisfied as they are with this form of government, that enforces taxation without representation—that compels them to obey laws to which they never have given their consent—that imprisons and hangs them without a trial by a jury of their peers—that robs them, in marriage, of the custody of their own persons, wages and children—are this half of the people who are left wholly at the mercy of the other half, in direct violation of the spirit and letter of the declarations of the framers of this government, every one of which was based on the immutable principle of equal rights to all. By these declarations, kings, popes, priests, aristocrats, all were alike dethroned and placed on a common level, politically, with the lowliest born subject or serf. By them, too, men, as such, were deprived of their divine right to rule and placed on a political level with women. By the practice of these declarations all class and caste distinctions would be abolished, and slave, serf, plebeian, wife, woman, all alike rise from their subject position to the broader platform of equality.

Constitutional Support for Woman's Right to Vote

The preamble of the Federal Constitution says:

> We, the people of the United States, in order to form a more perfect union, establish justice, insure domestic tranquillity, provide for the common defence, promote the general welfare and secure the blessings of liberty to ourselves and our posterity, do ordain and establish this Constitution for the United States of America.

It was we, the people, not we, the white male citizens, nor we, the male citizens; but we, the whole people, who formed this Union. We formed it not to give the blessings of liberty but to secure them; not to the half of ourselves and the half of our posterity, but to the whole people—women as well as men. It is downright mockery to talk to women of their enjoyment of the blessings of liberty while they are denied the only means of securing them provided by this democratic-republican government—the ballot.

The early journals of Congress show that, when the committee reported to that body the original articles of confederation, the very first one which became the subject of discussion was that respecting equality of suffrage. Article IV said:

> The better to secure and perpetuate mutual friendship and inter-
> course between the people of the different States of this Union,
> the free inhabitants of each of the States (paupers, vagabonds and
> fugitives from justice excepted) shall be entitled to all the privi-
> leges and immunities of the free citizens of the several States.

Thus, at the very beginning, did the Fathers see the necessity of the universal application of the great principle of
equal rights to all, in order to produce the desired result—a
harmonious union and a homogeneous people. . . .

No Grounds for Exclusion

I submit that in view of the explicit assertions of the equal
right of the whole people, both in the preamble and previous article of the constitution, this omission of the adjective
"female" should not be construed into a denial; but instead
should be considered as of no effect. Mark the direct prohibition, "No member of this state shall be disfranchised, unless by the law of the land, or the judgment of his peers."
"The law of the land" is the United States Constitution; and
there is no provision in that document which can be fairly
construed into a permission to the states to deprive any class
of citizens of their right to vote. Hence New York can get no
power from that source to disfranchise one entire half of her
members. Nor has "the judgment of their peers" been pronounced against women exercising their right to vote; no
disfranchised person is allowed to be judge or juror—and
none but disfranchised persons can be women's peers. Nor
has the legislature passed laws excluding women as a class
on account of idiocy or lunacy; nor have the courts con-
victed them of bribery, larceny or any infamous crime.
Clearly, then, there is no constitutional ground for the exclusion of women from the ballot-box in the state of New
York. No barriers whatever stand today between women and
the exercise of their right to vote save those of precedent and
prejudice, which refuse to expunge the word "male" from
the constitution.

The clauses of the United States Constitution cited by our
opponents as giving power to the States to disfranchise any

classes of citizens they please, are contained in Sections 2 and 4, Article I. The second says:

> The House of Representatives shall be composed of members chosen every second year by the people of the several States: and the electors in each State shall have the qualifications requisite for electors of the most numerous branch of the State legislature.

This can not be construed into a concession to the States of the power to destroy the right to become an elector, but simply to prescribe what shall be the qualifications, such as competency of intellect, maturity of age, length of residence, that shall be deemed necessary to enable them to make an intelligent choice of candidates. If, as our opponents assert, it is the duty of the United States to protect citizens in the several states against higher or different qualifications for electors for representatives in Congress than for members of the Assembly, then it must be equally imperative for the national government to interfere with the states, and forbid them from arbitrarily cutting off the right of one-half the people to become electors altogether. Section 4 says:

> The times, places and manner of holding elections for senators and representatives shall be prescribed in each State by the legislature thereof; but Congress may at any time, by law, make or alter such regulations, except as to the places of choosing senators.

Here is conceded to the States only the power to prescribe times, places and manner of holding the elections; and even with these Congress may interfere in all excepting the mere place of choosing senators. Thus, you see, there is not the slightest permission for the States to discriminate against the right of any class of citizens to vote. Surely, to regulate can not be to annihilate; to qualify can not be wholly to deprive. To this principle every true Democrat and Republican said amen, when applied to black men by Senator Charles Sumner in his great speeches from 1865 to 1869 for equal rights to all; and when, in 1871, I asked that senator to declare the power of the United States Constitution to protect women in their right to vote—as he had done for black men—he handed me a copy of all his speeches during that reconstruction period, and said:

> Put "sex" where I have "race" or "color," and you have here the best and strongest argument I can make for woman. There is not a doubt but women have the constitutional right to vote, and I will never vote for a Sixteenth Amendment to guarantee it to them. I voted for both the Fourteenth and Fifteenth under protest; would never have done it but for the pressing emergency of that hour; would have insisted that the power of the original Constitution to protect all citizens in the equal enjoyment of their rights should have been vindicated through the courts. But the newly-made freedmen had neither the intelligence, wealth nor time to await that slow process. Women do possess all these in an eminent degree, and I insist that they shall appeal to the courts, and through them establish the powers of our American magna charta to protect every citizen of the republic.

Putting Theory into Practice

But, friends, when in accordance with Senator Sumner's counsel I went to the ballot-box, last November, and exercised my citizen's right to vote, the courts did not wait for me to appeal to them—they appealed to me, and indicted me on the charge of having voted illegally. Putting sex where he did color, Senator Sumner would have said:

> Qualifications can not be in their nature permanent or insurmountable. Sex can not be a qualification any more than size, race, color or previous condition of servitude. A permanent or insurmountable qualification is equivalent to a deprivation of the suffrage. In other words, it is the tyranny of taxation without representation, against which our Revolutionary mothers, as well as fathers, rebelled.

For any state to make sex a qualification, which must ever result in the disfranchisement of one entire half of the people, is to pass a bill of attainder, an ex post facto law, and is therefore a violation of the supreme law of the land. By it the blessings of liberty are forever withheld from women and their female posterity. For them, this government has no just powers derived from the consent of the governed. For them this government is not a democracy; it is not a republic. It is the most odious aristocracy ever established on the face of the globe. An oligarchy of wealth, where the rich govern the poor; an oligarchy of learning, where the educated govern the ignorant; or even an oligarchy of race, where the Saxon rules the African, might be endured; but this oligarchy of sex which makes father, brothers, husband, sons, the oligarchs over the mother and sisters, the wife and daughters of every household; which ordains all men sovereigns, all women subjects—carries discord and rebellion into every home of the nation. This most odious aristocracy exists, too, in the face of Section 4, Article IV, which says: "The United States shall guarantee to every State in the Union a republican form of government."

What, I ask you, is the distinctive difference between the inhabitants of a monarchical and those of a republican form of government, save that in the monarchical the people are subjects, helpless, powerless, bound to obey laws made by political superiors; while in the republican the people are citizens, individual sovereigns, all clothed with equal power to make and unmake both their laws and law-makers? The moment you deprive a person of his right to a voice in the government, you degrade him from the status of a citizen of the republic to that of a subject. It matters very little to him whether his monarch be an individual tyrant, as is the Czar of Russia, or a 15,000,000 headed monster, as here in the United States; he is a powerless subject, serf or slave; not in any sense a free and independent citizen.

It is urged that the use of the masculine pronouns *he, his* and *him* in all the constitutions and laws, is proof that only men were meant to be included in their provisions. If you insist on this version of the letter of the law, we shall insist that you be consistent and accept the other horn of the dilemma, which would compel you to exempt women from taxation for the support of the government and from penalties for the violation of laws. There is no *she* or *her* or *hers* in the tax laws, and this is equally true of all the criminal laws.

Take for example the civil rights law which I am charged with having violated; not only are all the pronouns in it masculine, but everybody knows that it was intended expressly to hinder the rebel men from voting. It reads, "If any person shall knowingly vote without *his* having a lawful right." It was precisely so with all the papers served on me—the United States marshal's warrant, the bail-bond, the petition for habeas corpus, the bill of indictment—not one of them had a feminine pronoun; but to make them applicable to me, the clerk of the court prefixed an "s" to the "he" and made "her" out of "his" and "him;" and I insist if government officials may thus manipulate the pronouns to tax, fine, imprison and hang women, it is their duty to thus change them in order to protect us in our right to vote. . . .

Are Women Persons?

Though the words persons, people, inhabitants, electors, citizens, are all used indiscriminately in the national and state constitutions, there was always a conflict of opinion, prior to the war, as to whether they were synonymous terms, but whatever room there was for doubt, under the old regime, the adoption of the Fourteenth Amendment settled that question forever in its first sentence:

> All persons born or naturalized in the United States, and subject to the jurisdiction thereof, are citizens of the United States, and of the State wherein they reside.

The second settles the equal status of all citizens:

> No State shall make or enforce any law which shall abridge the privileges or immunities of citizens of the United States: nor shall any State deprive any person of life, liberty or property without due process of law, or deny to any person within its jurisdiction the equal protection of the laws.

The only question left to be settled now is: Are women persons? I scarcely believe any of our opponents will have the hardihood to say they are not. Being persons, then, women are citizens, and no state has a right to make any new law, or to enforce any old law, which shall abridge their privileges or immunities. Hence, every discrimination against women in the constitutions and laws of the several states is today null and void, precisely as is every one against negroes.

Is the right to vote one of the privileges or immunities of citizens? I think the disfranchised ex-rebels and ex-state prisoners all will agree that it is not only one of them, but the one without which all the others are nothing. Seek first the kingdom of the ballot and all things else shall be added, is the political injunction. . . .

If once we establish the false principle that United States citizenship does not carry with it the right to vote in every state in this Union, there is no end to the petty tricks and cunning devices which will be attempted to exclude one and another class of citizens from the right of suffrage. It will not always be the men combining to disfranchise all women; native born men combining to abridge the rights of all naturalized citizens, as in Rhode Island. It will not always be the rich and educated who may combine to cut off the poor and ignorant; but we may live to see the hard-working, uncultivated day laborers, foreign and native born, learning the power of the ballot and their vast majority of numbers, combine and amend state constitutions so as to disfranchise the Vanderbilts, the Stewarts, the Conklings and the Fentons. It is a poor rule that won't work more ways than one. Establish this precedent, admit the state's right to deny suffrage, and there is no limit to the confusion, discord and disruption that may await us. There is and can be but one safe principle of government—equal rights to all. Discrimination against any class on account of color, race, nativity, sex, property, culture, can but embitter and disaffect that class, and thereby endanger the safety of the whole people. Clearly, then, the national government not only must define the rights of citizens, but must stretch out its powerful hand and protect them in every state in this Union. . . .

A Call for Action

It is upon this just interpretation of the United States Constitution that our National Woman Suffrage Association, which celebrates the twenty-fifth anniversary of the woman's rights movement next May in New York City, has based all its arguments and action since the passage of these amendments. We no longer petition legislature or Congress to give us the right to vote, but appeal to women everywhere to exercise their too long neglected "citizen's right." We appeal to the inspectors of election to receive the votes of all United States citizens, as it is their duty to do. We appeal to United States commissioners and marshals to arrest, as is their duty, the inspectors who reject the votes of United States citizens, and leave alone those who perform their duties and accept these votes. We ask the juries to return verdicts of "not guilty" in the cases of law-abiding United States citizens who cast their votes, and inspectors of election who receive and count them.

We ask the judges to render unprejudiced opinions of the law, and where-ever there is room for doubt to give the benefit to the side of liberty and equal rights for women, remembering that, as Summer says, "The true rule of interpretation under our National Constitution, especially since its amendments, is that anything *for* human rights is constitutional, everything *against* human rights unconstitutional." It is on this line that we propose to fight our battle for the ballot—peaceably but nevertheless persistently—until we achieve complete triumph and all United States citizens, men and women alike, are recognized as equals in the government.

Citizenship Does Not Confer Voting Rights

U.S. Supreme Court

In 1872, Virginia Minor, the president of the Woman Suffrage Association of Missouri, adopted a confrontational strategy to secure the right of women to vote. Like several other prominent supporters of women's suffrage of the day (most notably, Susan B. Anthony), Minor registered to vote in the 1872 presidential election. Reese Happersett, a registrar of voters in Missouri, denied her request because she was not a male citizen of the United States, and, therefore, ineligible to vote under state laws. Minor sued Happersett because she alleged that his actions violated her constitutional right to vote as a citizen of the United States. The case was eventually appealed to the Supreme Court. The Supreme Court unanimously rejected the reasoning of Minor and her lawyers, thereby demonstrating that a separate constitutional amendment would be the only way to ensure suffrage for all American women.

The fourteenth amendment to the Constitution of the United States, in its first section, thus ordains:

> 'All persons born or naturalized in the United States, and subject to the jurisdiction thereof, are citizens of the United States, and of the State wherein they reside. No State shall make or enforce any law, which shall abridge the privileges or immunities of citizens of the United States. Nor shall any State deprive any person of life, liberty, or property, without due process of law; nor deny to any person within its jurisdiction, the equal protection of the laws.'

Excerpted from *Minor v. Happersett, 88 U.S. 162*, by the U.S. Supreme Court, http://laws.findlaw.com, 1874.

And the constitution of the State of Missouri thus ordains:

'Every male citizen of the United States shall be entitled to vote.'

Under a statute of the State all persons wishing to vote at any election, must previously have been registered in the manner pointed out by the statute, this being a condition precedent to the exercise of the elective franchise.

Summarizing the Facts of the Case

In this state of things, on the 15th of October, 1872 (one of the days fixed by law for the registration of voters), Mrs. Virginia Minor, a native born, free, white citizen of the United States, and of the State of Missouri, over the age of twenty-one years, wishing to vote for electors for President and Vice-President of the United States, and for a representative in Congress, and for other officers, at the general election held in November, 1872, applied to one Happersett, the registrar of voters, to register her as a lawful voter, which he refused to do, assigning for cause that she was not a 'male citizen of the United States,' but a woman. She thereupon sued him in one of the inferior State courts of Missouri, for willfully refusing to place her name upon the list of registered voters, by which refusal she was deprived of her right to vote.

The registrar demurred, and the court in which the suit was brought sustained the demurrer, and gave judgment in his favor; a judgment which the Supreme Court affirmed. Mrs. Minor now brought the case here on error. . . .

The CHIEF JUSTICE delivered the opinion of the court.

The question is presented in this case, whether, since the adoption of the fourteenth amendment, a woman, who is a citizen of the United States and of the State of Missouri, is a voter in that State, notwithstanding the provision of the constitution and laws of the State, which confine the right of suffrage to men alone. We might, perhaps, decide the case upon other grounds, but this question is fairly made. From the opinion we find that it was the only one decided in the court below, and it is the only one which has been argued here. The case was undoubtedly brought to this court for the sole purpose of having that question decided by us, and in view of the evident propriety there is of having it settled, so far as it can be by such a decision, we have concluded to waive all other considerations and proceed at once to its determination. . . .

Women Are Citizens, but Not Voters

There is no doubt that women may be citizens. They are persons, and by the fourteenth amendment 'all persons born or naturalized in the United States and subject to the jurisdiction thereof' are expressly declared to be 'citizens of the United States and of the State wherein they reside.' But, in our opinion, it did not need this amendment to give them that position. Before its adoption the Constitution of the United States did not in terms prescribe who should be citizens of the United States or of the several States, yet there were necessarily such citizens without such provision. There cannot be a nation without a people. The very idea of a political community, such as a nation is, implies an association of persons for the promotion of their general welfare. Each one of the persons associated becomes a member of the nation formed by the association. He owes it allegiance and is entitled to its protection. Allegiance and protection are, in this connection, reciprocal obligations. The one is a compensation for the other; allegiance for protection and protection for allegiance.

For convenience it has been found necessary to give a name to this membership. The object is to designate by a title the person and the relation he bears to the nation. For this purpose the words 'subject,' 'inhabitant,' and 'citizen' have been used, and the choice between them is sometimes made to depend upon the form of the government. Citizen is now more commonly employed, however, and as it has been considered better suited to the description of one living under a republican government, it was adopted by nearly all of the States upon their separation from Great Britain, and was afterwards adopted in the Articles of Confederation and in the

Constitution of the United States. When used in this sense, it is understood as conveying the idea of membership of a nation, and nothing more. . . .

Whoever, then, was one of the people of either of these States when the Constitution of the United States was adopted, became ipso facto a citizen—a member of the nation created by its adoption. He was one of the persons associating together to form the nation, and was, consequently, one of its original citizens. As to this there has never been a doubt. Disputes have arisen as to whether or not certain persons or certain classes of persons were part of the people at the time, but never as to their citizenship if they were. . . .

Sex has never been made one of the elements of citizenship in the United States. In this respect men have never had an advantage over women. The same laws precisely apply to both. The fourteenth amendment did not affect the citizenship of women any more than it did of men. In this particular, therefore, the rights of Mrs. Minor do not depend upon the amendment. She has always been a citizen from her birth, and entitled to all the privileges and immunities of citizenship. The amendment prohibited the State, of which she is a citizen, from abridging any of her privileges and immunities as a citizen of the United States; but it did not confer citizenship on her. That she had before its adoption.

If the right of suffrage is one of the necessary privileges of a citizen of the United States, then the constitution and laws of Missouri confining it to men are in violation of the Constitution of the United States, as amended, and consequently void. The direct question is, therefore, presented whether all citizens are necessarily voters.

The Constitution does not define the privileges and immunities of citizens. For that definition we must look elsewhere. In this case we need not determine what they are, but only whether suffrage is necessarily one of them. . . .

The [fourteenth] amendment did not add to the privileges and immunities of a citizen. It simply furnished an additional guarantee for the protection of such as he already had. No new voters were necessarily made by it. Indirectly it may have had that effect, because it may have increased the number of citizens entitled to suffrage under the constitution and laws of the States, but it operates for this purpose, if at all, through the States and the State laws, and not directly upon the citizen.

It is clear, therefore, we think, that the Constitution has not added the right of suffrage to the privileges and immunities of citizenship as they existed at the time it was adopted. This makes it proper to inquire whether suffrage was coextensive with the citizenship of the States at the time of its adoption. If it was, then it may with force be argued that suffrage was one of the rights which belonged to citizenship, and in the enjoyment of which every citizen must be protected. But if it was not, the contrary may with propriety be assumed.

A History of Restricting Women's Suffrage

When the Federal Constitution was adopted, all the States, with the exception of Rhode Island and Connecticut, had constitutions of their own. These two continued to act under their charters from the Crown. Upon an examination of those constitutions we find that in no State were all citizens permitted to vote. Each State determined for itself who should have that power. Thus, in New Hampshire, 'every male inhabitant of each town and parish with town privileges, and places unincorporated in the State, of twenty-one years of age and upwards, excepting paupers and persons excused from paying taxes at their own request,' were its voters; in Massachusetts 'every male inhabitant of twenty-one years of age and upwards, having a freehold estate within the commonwealth of the annual income of three pounds, or any estate of the value of sixty pounds;' in Rhode Island 'such as are admitted free of the company and society' of the colony; in Connecticut such persons as had 'maturity in years, quiet and peaceable behavior, a civil conversation, and forty shillings freehold or forty pounds personal estate,'[etc.]. . . .

In this condition of the law in respect to suffrage in the

several States it cannot for a moment be doubted that if it had been intended to make all citizens of the United States voters, the framers of the Constitution would not have left it to implication. So important a change in the condition of citizenship as it actually existed, if intended, would have been expressly declared. But if further proof is necessary to show that no such change was intended, it can easily be found both in and out of the Constitution. By Article 4, section 2, it is provided that 'the citizens of each State shall be entitled to all the privileges and immunities of citizens in the several States.' If suffrage is necessarily a part of citizenship, then the citizens of each State must be entitled to vote in the several States precisely as their citizens are. This is more than asserting that they may change their residence and become citizens of the State and thus be voters. It goes to the extent of insisting that while retaining their original citizenship they may vote in any State. This, we think, has never been claimed. And again, by the very terms of the amendment we have been considering (the fourteenth), 'Representatives shall be apportioned among the several States according to their respective numbers, counting the whole number of persons in each State, excluding Indians not taxed. But when the right to vote at any election for the choice of electors for President and Vice-President of the United States, representatives in Congress, the executive and judicial officers of a State, or the members of the legislature thereof, is denied to any of the male inhabitants of such State, being twenty-one years of age and citizens of the United States, or in any way abridged, except for participation in the rebellion, or other crimes, the basis of representation therein shall be reduced in the proportion which the number of such male citizens shall bear to the whole number of male citizens twenty-one years of age in such State.' Why this, if it was not in the power of the legislature to deny the right of suffrage to some male inhabitants? And if suffrage was necessarily one of the absolute rights of citizenship, why confine the operation of the limitation to male inhabitants? Women and children are, as we have seen, 'persons.' They are counted in the enumeration upon which the apportionment is to be made, but if they were necessarily voters because of their citizenship unless clearly excluded, why inflict the penalty for the exclusion of males alone? Clearly, no such form of words would have been selected to express the idea here indicated if suffrage was the absolute right of all citizens.

"We Are No Seditious Women"

Zerelda Wallace, the widow of a governor and member of Congress as well as the stepmother of General Lew Wallace, the author of Ben-Hur, testified on women's suffrage in front of Congress in 1880. Through her testimony she tries to allay the fears of some members of Congress who thought that granting women the right to vote would lead to demands for special rights for women. She also argues that granting the right to vote for women would increase the quality of political decisions.

That is the reason why we are here; that is the reason why we want to vote. We are no seditious women, clamoring for any peculiar rights, but we are patient women. It is not the woman question that brings us before you today; it is the human question that underlies this movement among the women of this nation; it is for God, and home, and native land. We love and appreciate our country; we value the institutions of our country. We realize that we owe great obligations to the men of this nation for what they have done. We realize that to their strength we owe the subjugation of all the material forces of the universe which gives us comfort and luxury in our homes. We realize that to their brains we owe the machinery that gives us leisure for intellectual culture and achievement. We realize that it is to their education we owe the opening of our colleges and the establishment of our public schools, which give us these great and glorious privileges.

This movement is the legitimate result of this development, of this enlightenment, and of the suffering that woman has undergone in the ages past. We find ourselves hedged in

And still again, after the adoption of the fourteenth amendment, it was deemed necessary to adopt a fifteenth, as follows: 'The right of citizens of the United States to vote shall not be denied or abridged by the United States, or by any State, on account of race, color, or previous condition of servitude.' The fourteenth amendment had already provided that no State should make or enforce any law which

---

at every effort we make as mothers for the amelioration of society, as philanthropists, as Christians.

A short time ago I went before the legislature of Indiana with a petition signed by 25,000 women, the best women in the State. I appeal to the memory of Judge McDonald to substantiate the truth of what I say. Judge McDonald knows that I am a home-loving, law-abiding, tax-paying woman of Indiana, and have been for fifty years. When I went before our legislature and found that one hundred of the vilest men in our State, merely by the possession of the ballot, had more influence with the law-makers of our land than the wives and mothers of the nation, it was a revelation that was perfectly startling.

You must admit that in popular government the ballot is the most potent means of all moral and social reforms. As members of society, as those who are deeply interested in the promotion of good morals, of virtue, and of the proper protection of men from the consequences of their own vices, and of the protection of women, too, we are deeply interested in all the social problems with which you have grappled so long unsuccessfully. We do not intend to depreciate your efforts, but you have attempted to do an impossible thing. You have attempted to represent the whole by one-half; and we come to you today for a recognition of the fact that humanity is not a unit; that it is a unity, and because we are one-half that go to make up that grand unity we come before you today and ask you to recognize our rights as citizens of this Republic.

Anne F. Scott and Andrew M. Scott, eds., *One Half the People: The Fight for Woman Suffrage*. Philadelphia, PA: J.B. Lippincott Company, 1975, p. 97.

should abridge the privileges or immunities of citizens of the United States. If suffrage was one of these privileges or immunities, why amend the Constitution to prevent its being denied on account of race, etc.? Nothing is more evident than that the greater must include the less, and if all were already protected why go through with the form of amending the Constitution to protect a part? . . .

Women were excluded from suffrage in nearly all the States by the express provision of their constitutions and laws. If that had been equivalent to a bill of attainder [a legislative trial], certainly its abrogation [abolishment] would not have been left to implication. Nothing less than express language would have been employed to effect so radical a change. So also of the amendment which declares that no person shall be deprived of life, liberty, or property without due process of law, adopted as it was as early as 1791. If suffrage was intended to be included within its obligations, language better adapted to express that intent would most certainly have been employed. The right of suffrage, when granted, will be protected. He who has it can only be deprived of it by due process of law, but in order to claim protection he must first show that he has the right.

But we have already sufficiently considered the proof found upon the inside of the Constitution. That upon the outside is equally effective.

The Constitution was submitted to the States for adoption in 1787, and was ratified by nine States in 1788, and finally by the thirteen original States in 1790. Vermont was the first new State admitted to the Union, and it came in under a constitution which conferred the right of suffrage only upon men of the full age of twenty-one years, having resided in the State for the space of one whole year next before the election, and who were of quiet and peaceable behavior. This was in 1791. The next year, 1792, Kentucky followed with a constitution confining the right of suffrage to free male citizens of the age of twenty-one years who had resided in the State two years or in the county in which they offered to vote one year next before the election. . . . No new

State has ever been admitted to the Union which has conferred the right of suffrage upon women, and this has never been considered a valid objection to her admission. On the contrary, as is claimed in the argument, the right of suffrage was withdrawn from women as early as 1807 in the State of New Jersey, without any attempt to obtain the interference of the United States to prevent it. Since then the governments of the insurgent States [the states of the Confederacy during the Civil War] have been reorganized under a requirement that before their representatives could be admitted to seats in Congress they must have adopted new constitutions, republican in form. In no one of these constitutions was suffrage conferred upon women, and yet the States have all been restored to their original position as States in the Union. . . .

Certainly, if the courts can consider any question settled, this is one. For nearly ninety years the people have acted upon the idea that the Constitution, when it conferred citizenship, did not necessarily confer the right of suffrage. If uniform practice long continued can settle the construction of so important an instrument as the Constitution of the United States confessedly is, most certainly it has been done here. Our province is to decide what the law is, not to declare what it should be.

The Law May Be Wrong, but It Is Clear

We have given this case the careful consideration its importance demands. If the law is wrong, it ought to be changed; but the power for that is not with us. The arguments addressed to us bearing upon such a view of the subject may perhaps be sufficient to induce those having the power, to make the alteration, but they ought not to be permitted to influence our judgment in determining the present rights of the parties now litigating before us. No argument as to woman's need of suffrage can be considered. We can only act upon her rights as they exist. It is not for us to look at the hardship of withholding. Our duty is at an end if we find it is within the power of a State to withhold.

Being unanimously of the opinion that the Constitution of the United States does not confer the right of suffrage upon any one, and that the constitutions and laws of the several States which commit that important trust to men alone are not necessarily void, we
    AFFIRM THE JUDGMENT.

Debating Women's Suffrage in Congress

U.S. Senate

In 1874, the U.S. Senate debated the establishment of a new territory, Pembina (which eventually became the Dakota Territory). Part of the Senate's task was to decide the form of government that would rule over this new territory. Senator Aaron Sargent of California proposed that all inhabitants, male and female, should be allowed to vote in elections in this new territory. His proposal sparked a larger debate about the desirability of women's suffrage throughout the entire United States. The senators' debate presents a wide array of arguments on both sides of this highly contentious issue—illustrating the difficult road that supporters of women's suffrage faced.

Mr. BOREMAN. I move to proceed with the consideration of the bill to establish the Territory of Pembina, and to provide a temporary government therefor. . . .

Mr. SARGENT. I move to add to line 10 of section 5 the word "sex.". . .

The CHIEF CLERK. If the amendment be adopted, the clause will then read:

> *Provided*, That the Legislative Assembly shall not, at any time, abridge the right of suffrage, or to hold office, on account of sex, race, color, or previous condition of servitude of any resident of the Territory.

Mr. SARGENT. I believe, Mr. President, that the amendment which I offer to this bill is justified by the organic law

Excerpted from *Congressional Record and Appendix: Forty-Third Congress, First Session*, by the U.S. Senate, 1874.

of the United States, and in fact required by that law. Before the adoption of the fourteenth and fifteenth articles of amendment to the Constitution of the United States women were hedged out of the ballot-box by the use of the word "male." Since that time another rule has been prescribed by the organic law, and it is made the right of all citizens of the United States to approach the ballot-box and exercise this highest privilege of a citizen. By the fourteenth article of amendment it is provided that "all persons born or naturalized in the United States, and subject to the jurisdiction thereof, are citizens of the United States and of the State wherein they reside." This most important declaration is now the organic law of the United States. It does not say "all males born or naturalized in the United States," but "all persons," and it cannot be contended successfully that a woman is not a person, and not a person within the meaning of this clause of the Constitution. . . .

I believe that by realizing the intention of the Constitution, which uses words that are so fully explained by our courts and by our writers upon the uses of words, we simply open a wider avenue to women for usefulness to themselves and to society. I think we give them an opportunity, instead of traveling the few and confined roads that are open to them now, to engage more generally in the business of life under some guarantee of their success. I believe that, instead of driving them to irregular efforts like those which they recently have made in many of the States to overthrow liquor selling and consumption and its desolation of their homes, it will give them an opportunity through the ballot-box to protect their families, to break up the nefarious traffic, and purify society. As it is now, their energies in this direction are repressed, and sometimes in order to have force are compelled to be exercised even in opposition to law. I would give them an opportunity to exercise them under the forms of law, and I would enforce the law by the accession of this pure element. I do not think that they would be corrupted by it, but rather that society and politics and your laws would be purified by admitting them to the ballot-box and giving them this opportunity. . . .

A Worthy Experiment

Mr. STEWART. If this region is to be created into a Territory, I think it eminently proper that this amendment should be adopted. The question of female suffrage is a question that is being seriously considered by a large portion of the people of the United States. We may think lightly of it here; we may think it never will be accomplished; but there are a great many earnest people who believe if females had the ballot they could better protect themselves, be more independent, and occupy useful positions in life which are now denied to them. Whether they be correct or not, it is not necessary for us to determine in passing upon this amendment. Here is a new Territory to be created and it is a good opportunity to try this experiment. If it works badly, when the Territory becomes a state there is nobody committed. . . .

If it works well, if it succeeds in protecting females in their rights and enabling them to assert their rights elsewhere and obtain such employment as is suitable to them, I hope it will become catching and spread all over the country, if that is the light in which it is to be treated. I am in earnest about this matter. I think this new Territory is the place to try the experiment right here. If it works badly, we can see it and no great harm will be done. If it works well, the example will be a good one and will be imitated. . . .

All Men Are Created Equal

Mr. MORTON. I am in favor of the amendment upon what I regard as the fundamental principles of our Government, upon the theory upon which we have based our Government from the beginning. The Declaration of Independence says:

> We hold these truths to be self-evident, that all men are created equal; that they are endowed by their Creator with certain unalienable rights; that among these are life, liberty, and the pursuit of happiness.

The word "men" in that connection does not mean males, but it means the human family; that all human beings are created equal. This will hardly be denied. . . . It embraces both sexes; not simply males, but females. All human beings are created equal. That is the foundation principle of our government. . . .

If these rights are fundamental, if they belong to all human beings as such, if they are God-given rights, then all persons having these God-given rights have a right to use the means for their preservation. The means is Government: "To secure these rights, governments are instituted among men, deriving their just powers from the consent of the governed."

I ask you whether the women of this country have ever given their consent to this government? Have they the means of giving their consent to it? . . . You say they are consenting. I say they are assenting to it, the majority of them; but they have no means of giving their consent to this government within the theory of the Declaration of Independence; and they cannot consent to it unless they have a voice, have a right to vote "yes" or to vote "no." . . .

This idea that women will be degraded by allowing them to go to the polls comes down to us from other countries and from remote periods of civilization. Why, sir, in countries now that claim to be civilized it is said that to allow the wife or the mother to go to the dinner-table with the husband and meet his guests face to face degrades her and degrades them. In some countries a woman must not appear upon the streets unless she is so closely veiled that she cannot be recognized; for it is said to allow her to go upon the streets barefaced or so thinly veiled that she can be recognized, subjects her to insult and degrades her; and in some countries to-day it destroys her character as effectually as other things would destroy her character in our country.

We know that is a prejudice; and the idea that woman will be degraded by giving her the right of suffrage is a remnant of that same idea. It is born of the same parentage. It has no sounder reason for it than these other nations have. I believe that to give women the right of suffrage would elevate the character of suffrage in this country. It would make the polls more decent, more respectable than they are now. Why, sir, fifty years ago the idea of women attending political meetings was intolerable to a great many people. The idea of her going to lectures of a scientific character was thought to be out of all reason. But now women go to political meetings. In almost every canvass in my State there are nearly as many women who attend the meetings as men. What is the effect of it? Are they degraded? On the contrary, their presence elevates the character of those meetings. It is an assurance of peace, it is a security against rowdyism and violence, because in this country men have to be very low if they are guilty of rowdyism or blackguardism in the presence of women. . . . When a woman is allowed to go to the polls and vote her sentiments and convictions, it will have the same effect there that her presence has in society. There is not a bit of doubt about it. And there will be no more discord in the family circle than there was when in violation and against the old principles of the common law you gave a woman the right to retain her legal existence after marriage and to own property separate and apart from her husband. These old notions have been giving way one after another little by little, and we shall finally come down to the true theory of our government in all respects, and that is to allow every person, man or woman, who is to be affected and controlled by the Government, whose interest or whose happiness is to be controlled by or depends on the administration of that Government, to have an equal voice in that government. Therefore I give my vote heartily and cheerfully for this amendment. . . .

Women Do Not Want to Vote

Mr. MERRIMON. Mr. President, I will not yield to any Senator in the measure of my respect for and admiration of woman; I do not propose by any act or word of mine to detract from her dignity or to diminish the pleasures she may enjoy in this life; but I claim the right to be the judge, in conjunction with herself, of what is best calculated to elevate and protect her dignity and promote her happiness. I do not believe that woman herself believes that her dignity would be elevated or her happiness promoted by putting her upon an exact equality, civilly or politically, in both points of view, with man; and very strong and controlling evidence of that fact is, that neither in this country nor in any country has woman—I mean the great mass of them—ever demanded such a state of things. Our Government has existed for about a hundred years, and the number of females who have demanded to be invested with equal political and civil rights and to be placed upon an exact equality with the male portion of our population, compared with those who have remained in retirement, who have staid at their homes and lived and ruled within that sphere in which it seems God intended that they should rule, is as a drop in the sea. So it appears in this conclusive way that the women of America do not demand this state of things. They do not protect themselves by votes, nor do they need to do so. They shape the man when he is a child, rule him with the power of love, and thus they shape, affect, and often control the destinies of men, nations, and empires. They rule in the domestic and moral world, and their invincible weapon is the power of holy love. . . .

Men Will Benefit

Mr. CARPENTER. Mr. President, . . . I desire to say one word as to the reason why I shall so vote [for suffrage].

I believe it is not one of woman's rights, but it is one of man's, that the franchise should be extended to women. I believe there is no situation in which man can be placed where the aid of woman is not beneficial. . . . Look through your country, look in your railroad cars, look in your post-offices, look in your dry-goods stores, and there you see everything decent and orderly and quiet. Why? Because women go there. The only place in this country from which they are excluded by law is the voting place, and in many of our large cities those places are the most disgraceful that can be found under our institutions. Now, I believe if the elections were open to ladies as well as gentlemen, to women as well as men, there would be as much order, quiet, and decency at the voting places as there is in a railroad car, and for precisely the same reason. If our wives and mothers and daughters were going to these election places there would be order and decency there, or there would be a row once for all that would make them decent. . . .

A Political Right Is a Man's Right

Mr. MORRILL, of Maine. Mr. President, I shall vote against this amendment, and for the reason that I do not consider the right of suffrage a woman's right or a man's right. I do not understand it to be a natural right at all. It is a political right; and I do not understand, as applied to women, that it is a privilege at all. It is akin to a service; and it is a very rough service. It is in its nature akin to militia service. The man who exercises the ballot must be prepared to defend it with the bayonet; and therefore the propriety of its being confined in all ages to men. . . .

My honorable friend from Wisconsin [Senator Carpenter] says there is no position in life in which the society of woman would not be an improvement. How is it on the deck of a battle-ship? How is it in military affairs? Should she be placed in the militia to enforce the results of a ballot? Is there any of us who believe that? Is there anybody here who would be glad to see a woman in the train-band, on the muster-field, at the cannon's mouth, or on the decks of your war-ships? That is what your argument means, if it means anything logically.

But, sir, I am not going to argue the proposition at all. I am going to vote against it because the right of suffrage is that rugged and severe service which man has no right to devolve upon woman. It is enough to say that when the American women want the ballot, when they come to hanker for it, and fall in love with the exercise of the ballot at the polls, I am in favor of their voting, but not until then; and I am not in favor of that sentimental sort of stuff which is gotten up somewhere or other by portions of the people who would force it upon the American women as a general proposition. Whenever they come to desire it, whenever the American women come to ask it, and particularly when they come to demand it, or even to solicit it, there will be no question as to what the American Congress will do; but until that time comes I shall vote steadily against it. . . .

I Appeal for the Women

Mr. SARGENT. I have no doubt of the consistency of my friend from Maine [Senator Morrill] on this proposition and on every other; but I differ with him upon both the propositions which he advances. He says that women do not desire the right of suffrage and there is no evidence before Congress that they do desire it. Why, sir, the tables of your committee-rooms have been loaded with petitions from every state in this Union on this subject, and they come forward day after day.

Mr. EDMUNDS. And remonstrances [protests] also.

Mr. SARGENT. Very few indeed. . . .

But the fact that there are remonstrances against the extension of the suffrage to women shows that there is agitation, and agitation shows interest in the matter. If this opinion were not in danger of prevailing, if it were not sweeping over the country, we would get no remonstrances; it would be looked upon as mere idle wind blowing nowhere and amounting to nothing. . . .

It is not for the few women who remonstrate from luxurious parlors, sitting upon sofas, in the glare of the gaslight, changing and choosing their phrases, but for the great class of laboring women in the country that I appeal for this redress. I appeal for the women who have been struggling on in these government offices, doing the same work that men do, ay, and in many cases doing it better, for about one-half of the pay. Do you suppose if they had ballots they would not make their voices heard here and get for the same work the same pay? Who ever knew a labor strike of women to succeed? When women in New York City and other places are bowed down to the earth by their labor—making shirts at a shilling a day—and they strike for more pay, for more bread, for an opportunity to live, who ever heard of one of their strikes succeeding? Men strike from their workshops and they succeed, and why? Because they have the ballot;

because they have political force; because they have the power of citizenship behind them in its fullest sense. Give these poor struggling women the same chance and they can make their way to a fair remuneration of wages in the public offices, and they can make their way in the workshops, and these toiling mothers, widows, and sisters supporting orphan brothers and sisters will have some opportunity to vindicate their rights and to procure not merely political rights, but a chance to live, and a chance to avoid infamy. . . .

A House Divided Against Itself

Mr. BAYARD. Under the operation of this amendment what will become of the family, what will become of the family hearthstone around which cluster the very best influences of human education? You will have a family with two heads— a "house divided against itself." You will no longer have that healthful and necessary subordination of wife to husband, and that unity of relationship which is required by a true and a real Christian marriage. You will have substituted a system of contention and difference warring against the laws of nature herself, and attempting by these new-fangled, petty, puny, and most contemptible contrivances, organized in defiance of the best lessons of human experience, to confuse, impede, and disarrange the palpable will of the Creator of the world. I can see in this proposition for female suffrage the end of all that home-life and education which are the best nursery for a nation's virtue. I can see in all these attempts to invade the relations between man and wife, to establish differences, to declare those to be two whom God hath declared to be one, elements of chaotic disorder, elements of destruction to all those things which are, after all, our best reliance for a good and a pure and an honest government. . . .

A Sign of Progress

Mr. STEWART. Now I undertake to say that there is no surer criterion of the civilization of any nation than the position which woman occupies; and the less dependent she is the more she has to do with the management of society, the more she is regarded as an individual, the higher that society stands, and you may take any place you please to illustrate; but where she depends exclusively on man and man's justice, there you have absolute barbarism. . . .

I do believe that if the good women of America could speak to-day they would reform many evils that we wink at or allow to exist because we want the votes of the parties who are committing these sins against society. I say let the women have a voice; and when it is said that this is ill-considered, that this is not the proper time, and that it is too serious a business to be considered by the Senate of the United States on this bill, I tell you society is marching on to it, and as I remarked before it will not be ten years before there will be no voice in this Senate against female suffrage. It is necessary for women, if they are to be protected in society and not to be the prey of man, that they shall have the ballot to protect themselves. It is the only thing in a free government that can protect any one; and whether it is a natural right or an artificial right it is nonsense to discuss. It is a necessary right; it is necessary to freedom; it is necessary to equal rights; it is necessary to protection; it is necessary for every class to have the ballot if we are going to have a square deal and equal rights. . . .

The PRESIDING OFFICER, (Mr. ANTHONY in the chair.) The question is on the amendment of the Senator from California, [Mr. SARGENT,] upon which the yeas and nays have been ordered.

The Secretary proceeded to call the roll.

The roll-call having been concluded, the result was announced—yeas 19, nays 27. . . .

So the amendment was rejected.

Chapter 3

Campaigning in the States

Chapter Preface

From 1875 until 1913, the women's suffrage movement proceeded with the understanding that the only way it would be successful was to convince each state separately that it should grant women the right to vote. The work was often tiring, time-consuming, and expensive. Speakers logged thousands of miles of travel (by stagecoach, horseback, riverboat, train, and car) to present their ideas to often-hostile crowds. Unfortunately, their hard work did not regularly pay off. From 1870 until 1910, only four states granted women the right to vote, despite the fact that there were nearly five hundred different campaigns in more than thirty states.

One problem was the less-than-optimal conditions under which the supporters of women's suffrage often worked. For example, in 1890, the women's suffrage movement turned its attention to South Dakota, which was debating whether to grant women the right to vote. Unfortunately, the summer of 1890 was the hottest and driest summer on record. Speakers would grow tired while riding twenty miles between the afternoon and evening meetings (and those attending the talks would themselves have traveled as many miles). Despite the efforts of Susan B. Anthony and other prominent women's suffrage leaders who traversed the sparsely populated state for several months in 1890, the amendment failed by a two-to-one margin. South Dakota continued to be an exhausting and frustrating state to convince. In total, it took five separate campaigns—and twenty-eight years—before South Dakota would grant its female population the right to vote.

Another challenge in the battle for state recognition of women's suffrage was the consistent struggle for sufficient funds to mount any sort of effective campaign. For example, when the 1893 campaign for women's suffrage started in Colorado, the treasury of that state's women's suffrage association had only twenty-five dollars. The rest came from small donations that the suffrage speakers collected as they campaigned around the state. These efforts were modestly successful and eventually raised two thousand dollars. Because of such a limited set of funds, suffrage campaigns by necessity relied heavily on volunteer work. The Colorado organization was extremely thrifty; it spent only seventeen dollars on election day. In the end, though, it was successful. On November 7, the voters helped Colorado become the second state to grant women the right to vote. Even so, the constant need for funds was one that would plague the various state-level campaigns.

A final obstacle in the state campaigns was the often virulent opposition suffragists faced. Some of the animosity stemmed from a strong belief that women should not become involved in the rough-and-tumble world of politics. Other men, however, objected because they felt that their livelihood would be threatened if women were allowed to vote. Saloonkeepers and others involved in the liquor industry were especially fearful. They reasoned that if women were enfranchised, they would heavily favor the growing calls for the prohibition against the sale and consumption of alcohol. These fears were not entirely unfounded. Many suffragists were actively involved in the temperance movement as well. To protect their economic interests, the liquor industry spent considerable time and money campaigning against women's suffrage. Many suffragists believed that the liquor lobby would not be above using unscrupulous methods if their money failed to sway voters. Some women were convinced that liquor interests instigated vote fraud to block the campaign to give women the right to vote.

Obtaining Women's Suffrage in Wyoming

J.W. Kingman

> In 1869, the Wyoming Territory became the first part of the
> United States to allow women to vote in all elections (some
> states had by then allowed women to vote in local matters such
> as school board elections). In their collection of suffrage writ-
> ings called *History of Woman Suffrage*, Elizabeth Cady Stan-
> ton, Susan B. Anthony, and Matilda Joslyn Gage called upon
> J.W. Kingman, an associate justice for the Wyoming Territory,
> to narrate the story of how suffrage was extended to women in
> Wyoming. In Kingman's view, the addition of women voters
> had a positive impact on the first elections in which Wyoming
> women were legally allowed to cast ballots. Kingman also
> describes how the Democrats in the Wyoming legislature were
> nearly able to overturn this law, but their efforts were thwarted
> by Wyoming's Republican governor, who vetoed their bill
> designed to outlaw women's suffrage.
>
> Wyoming maintained its historical role in women's suf-
> frage by becoming the first state in the Union to grant women
> the right to vote when it gained statehood in 1890. To com-
> memorate this achievement, Wyoming adopted the nickname
> "The Equality State."

After recording such a long succession of disappoint-
ments and humiliations for women in all the States in
their worthy endeavors for higher education, for profitable
employment in the trades and professions and for equal so-

Excerpted from *History of Woman Suffrage*, vol. 3, edited by Elizabeth Cady Stanton, Susan B. Anthony, and Matilda Joslyn Gage (Rochester, NY: Charles Mann, 1889).

cial, civil and political rights, it is with renewed self-respect and a stronger hope of better days to come that we turn to the magnificent territory of Wyoming, where the foundations of the first true republic were laid deep and strong in equal rights to all, and where for the first time in the history of the race woman has been recognized as a sovereign in her own right—an independent, responsible being—endowed with the capacity for self-government. This great event in the history of human progress transpired in 1869. . . .

The Story of Wyoming Suffrage

The successive steps by which this was accomplished are given us by Hon. J.W. Kingman, associate-justice in the territory for several years:

It is now sixteen years since the act was passed giving women the right to vote at all elections in this territory, including all the rights of an elector, with the right to hold office. The language of the statute is broad, and beyond the reach of evasion. It is as follows:

That every woman of the age of twenty-one years, residing in the territory, may, at every election to be holden under the laws thereof, cast her vote; and her rights to the elective franchise, and to hold office, shall be the same, under the election laws of the territory, as those of the electors.

There was no half-way work about it, no quibbling, no grudgingly parting with political power, no fear of consequences, but a manly acknowledgment of equal rights and equal privileges, among all the citizens of the new territory. . . .

The people of Wyoming have prospered under these laws, and are growing to like them better and better, and adapt themselves more and more to their provisions. The object of this sketch is to trace the progress and development of this new legislation, and gather up some of its consequences as they have been observed in our social and political relations.

The territory of Wyoming was first organized in May, 1869. The Union Pacific railroad was completed on the 9th of the month, and the transcontinental route opened to the public. There were but few people in the territory at that time, except such as had been brought hither in connection with the building of that road, and

In fact, he venerated his wife, and submitted to her judgment and influence more willingly than one could have supposed; and she was in favor of woman suffrage.[1] There were a few other men in that legislature, whose wives exercised a similar influence; but Mr. Bright found it up-hill work to get a majority for his bill, and it dragged along until near the close of the session. The character of the arguments he used, and the means he employed to win success are perhaps worthy of notice, as showing the men he had to deal with. I ought to say distinctly, that Mr. Bright was himself fully and firmly convinced of the justice and policy of his bill, and gave his whole energy and influence to secure its passage; he secured some members by arguing to support their pet schemes in return, and some he won over by even less creditable means. He got some votes by admitting that the governor would veto the bill (and it was generally understood that he would), insisting at the same time, that it would give the Democrats an advantage in future elections by showing that they were in favor of liberal measures while the Republican governor and the Republican party were opposed

---

1. Ex-Governor Hoyt in his public speeches frequently gives this bird's-eye view of Bright's domestic and political discussions: "Betty, it's a shame that I should be a member of the legislature and make laws for such a woman as you. You are a great deal better than I am; you know a great deal more, and you would make a better member of the Assembly than I, and you know it. I have been thinking about it and have made up my mind that I will go to work and do everything in my power to give you the ballot. Then you may work out the rest in your own way." So he went over and talked with other members of the legislature. They smiled. But he got one of the lawyers to help him draw up a short bill, which he introduced. It was considered and discussed. People smiled generally. There was not much expectation that anything of that sort would be done; but this was a shrewd fellow, who managed the party card in such a way as to get, as he believed, enough votes to carry the measure before it was brought to the test. I will show you a little behind the curtain, so far as I can draw it. Thus he said to the Democrats: "We have a Republican governor and a Democratic Assembly. Now, then, if we can carry this bill through the Assembly and the governor vetoes it, we shall have made a point, you know; we shall have shown our liberality and lost nothing. But keep still; don't say anything about it." They promised. He then went to the Republicans and told them that the Democrats were going to support his measure, and that if *they* did not want to lose capital they had better vote for it too. He didn't think there would be enough of them to carry it, but the vote would be on record and thus defeat the game of the other party. And they likewise agreed to vote for it. So when the bill came to a vote it went right through! The members looked at each other in astonishment, for they hadn't intended to do it, *quite.* Then they laughed and said it was a good joke, but they had "got the governor in a fix." So the bill went, in the course of time, to John A. Campbell, who was then governor—the first governor of the territory of Wyoming—and he promptly signed it! His heart was right. He saw that it was long-deferred justice, and so signed it as gladly as Abraham Lincoln wrote *his* name to the Proclamation of Emancipation of the slaves. Of course the women were astounded! If a whole troop of angels had come down with flaming swords for their vindication, they would not have been much more astonished than they were when that bill became a law and the women of Wyoming were thus clothed with the habiliments of citizenship.

to them. The favorite argument, however, and by far the most effective, was this: it would prove a great advertisement, would
make a great deal of talk, and attract attention to the legislature,
and the territory, more effectually than anything else. The bill was
finally passed and sent to the governor. I must add, however, that
many letters were written from different parts of the territory, and
particularly by the women, to members of the legislature, urging
its passage and approving its object.

On receipt of the bill, the governor was in great doubt what course
to take. He was inclined to veto it, and had so expressed himself;
but he did not like to take the responsibility of offending the
women in the territory, or of placing the Republican party in open
hostility to a measure which he saw might become of political
force and importance. . . . But in the end he signed it, and drew
upon himself the bitter curses of those Democrats who had voted
for the bill with the expectation that he would veto it. From this
time onward, the measure became rather a Republican than a
Democratic principle, and found more of its friends in the former
party, and more of its enemies in the latter. . . .

The First Election with Woman Suffrage

The first election under the woman suffrage law was held in September, 1870, for the election of a delegate in congress, and
county officers. There was an exciting canvass, and both parties
applied to the whisky shops, as before, supposing they would
wield the political power of the territory, and that not enough
women would vote to influence the result. The morning of election came, but did not bring the usual scenes around the polls. A
few women came out early to vote, and the crowd kept entirely
out of sight. There was plenty of drinking and noise at the saloons,
but the men would not remain, after voting, around the polls. It
seemed more like Sunday than election day. Even the negro men
and women voted without objection or disturbance. Quite a number of women voted during the day, at least in all the larger towns,
but apprehension of a repetition of the scenes of the former election, and doubt as to the proper course for them to pursue, kept
very many from voting. . . . I cannot deny myself the pleasure of
quoting at length the following letter of the Rev. D.J. Pierce, at
that time a resident of Laramie City, and a very wealthy man, to
show the powerful influence that was exerted on the mind of a
New England clergyman by that first exhibition of women at the

polls, and as evidence of the singular and beneficial change in the character of the election, and the conduct of the men.

Editor Laramie Sentinel: I am pleased to notice your action in printing testimonials of different classes to the influence of woman suffrage in Wyoming. With the apathy of conservatism and prejudice of party spirit arrayed against the idea in America, it is the duty of the residents in Wyoming to note the simple facts of their noted experiment, and lay them before the world for its consideration. I came from the vicinity of Boston, arriving in Laramie two weeks before the first regular election of 1870. I had never sympathized with the extreme theories of the woman's rights platform, to the advocates of which I had often listened in Boston. But I had never been able to learn just why a woman is naturally excluded from the privilege of franchise, and I sometimes argued in favor in lyceum [an organization that hosts public programs] debates. Still the question of her degradation stared me in the face, and I came to Wyoming unsettled in the matter, determined to be an impartial judge. I was early at the polls, but too late to witness the polling of the first female vote—by "Grandma" Swain, a much-esteemed Quaker lady of 75 summers, who determined by her words and influence to rally her sex to defend the cause of morality and justice.

I saw the rough mountaineers maintaining the most respectful decorum whenever the women approached the polls, and heard the timely warning of one of the leading canvassers as he silenced an incipient quarrel with uplifted finger, saying, "Hist! Be quiet! A woman is coming!"

And I was compelled to allow that in this new country, supposed at that time to be infested by hordes of cut-throats, gamblers and abandoned characters, I had witnessed a more quiet election than it had been my fortune to see in the quiet towns of Vermont. I saw ladies attended by their husbands, brothers, or sweethearts, ride to the places of voting, and alight in the midst of a silent crowd, and pass through an open space to the polls, depositing their votes with no more exposure to insult or injury than they would expect on visiting a grocery store or meat-market. Indeed, they were much safer here, every man of their party was pledged to shield them, while every member of the other party feared the influence of any signs of disrespect.

And the next day I sent my impressions to an eastern paper, declaring myself convinced that women's presence at the polls would elevate the tone of public sentiment there as it does in churches, the social hall, or any other place, while her own

robes are unspotted by the transcient association with evil characters which she is daily obliged to meet in the street or dry-
goods store. . . .

D.J. PIERCE, *Pastor Baptist Church.*

Efforts to Overturn Woman Suffrage

The legislature was strongly Democratic. There were four Republicans and five Democrats in the Council, and four Republicans and nine Democrats in the House. When they met in November, 1871, many Democrats were found to be bitterly opposed
to woman suffrage and determined to repeal the act; they said it
was evident they were losing ground and the Republicans gaining
by reason of the women voting, and that it must be stopped. The
Republicans were all inclined to sustain the law. Several caucuses
were held by the Democrats to determine on their course of action
and overcome the opposition in their own ranks. These caucuses
were held in one of the largest drinking saloons in Cheyenne and
all the power of whiskey was brought to bear on the members to
secure a repeal of the woman suffrage act. It required considerable time and a large amount of whiskey, but at last the opposition
was stifled and the Democratic party was brought up solid for repeal. A bill was introduced in the House for the purpose, but was
warmly resisted by the Republicans and a long discussion followed. It was finally carried by a strict party vote and sent to the
Council, where it met with the same opposition and the same result followed. It then went to the governor for his approval. There
was no doubt in his mind as to the course he ought to take. He had
seen the effects produced by the act of enfranchisement, and un-
hesitatingly approved all of them. He promptly returned the bill
with his veto; and the accompanying message is such an able paper and so fully sets forth the reasons in favor of the original act,
and the good results of its operation, that at least at few extracts
well deserve a prominent place in this record:

> I return herewith to the House of Representatives, in which it
> originated, a bill for "An Act to repeal Chapter XXXI. of the
> Laws of the First Legislative Assembly of the Territory of
> Wyoming."

> I regret that a sense of duty compels me to dissent from your
> honorable body with regard to any contemplated measure of
> public policy. It would certainly be more in accordance with
> the desire I have to secure and preserve the most harmonious
> relations among all the branches of our territorial government,

to approve the bill. A regard, however, for the rights of those whose interests are to be affected by it, and for what I believe to be the best interests of the territory, will not allow me to do so. The consideration, besides, that the passage of this bill would be, on the part of those instrumental in bringing it about, a declaration that the principles upon which the enfranchisement of women is urged are false and untenable, and that our experience demonstrates this, influences me not a little in my present action. . . .

The law granting to women the right to vote and to hold office in this territory was a natural and logical sequence to the other laws upon our statute-book. Our laws give to the widow the guardianship of her minor children. Will you take from her all voice in relation to the public schools established for the education of those children? Our laws permit women to acquire and possess property. Will you forbid them having any voice in relation to the taxation of that property? This bill says too little or too much. Too little, if you legislate upon the assumption that woman is an inferior who should be kept in a subordinate position, for in that case the other laws affecting her should be repealed or amended; and too much, if she is, as no one will deny, the equal of man in heart and mind, for in that case we cannot afford to dispense with her counsel and assistance in the government of the territory. . . .

Urged by all these considerations of right, and justice, and expediency, and the strong conviction of duty, I approved that act of which this bill contemplates the repeal, and it became a law. To warrant my reconsidering that action, there ought to be in the experience of the last two years something to show that the reasons upon which it was founded were unsound, or that the law itself was wrong or at least unwise and inexpedient. My view of the teachings of this experience is the very reverse of this. Women have voted, and have the officers chosen been less faithful and zealous and the legislature less able and upright? They have sat as jurors, and have the laws been less faithfully and justly administered, and criminals less promptly and adequately punished? Indeed the lessons of this two years' experience fully confirm all that has been claimed by the most ardent advocate of this innovation.

In this territory women have manifested for its highest interests a devotion strong, ardent, and intelligent. They have brought to public affairs a clearness of understanding and a soundness of judgment, which, considering their exclusion hitherto from practical participation in political agitations and movements, are worthy of the greatest admiration and above all praise. The conscience of women is in all things more discriminating and sensitive than that of men; their sense of justice, not compromising or time-serving, but pure and exacting; their love of order, not spasmodic or sentimental merely, but springing from the heart; all these,—the better conscience, the exalted sense of justice, and the abiding love of order, have been made by the enfranchisement of women to contribute to the good government and well-being of our territory. To the plain teachings of these two years' experience I cannot close my eyes. I cannot forget the benefits that have already resulted to our territory from woman suffrage, nor can I permit myself even to seem to do so by approving this bill. . . .

These were no hastily formed conclusions, but the result of deliberation and conviction, and my judgment to-day approves the language I then used. For the first time in the history of our country we have a government to which the noble words of our *Magna Charta* of freedom may be applied,—not as a mere figure of speech, but as expressing a simple grand truth,—for it is a government which "derives all its just powers from the consent of the governed." We should pause long and weigh carefully the probable results of our action before consenting to change this government. A regard for the genius of our institutions, for the fundamental principles of American autonomy, and for the immutable principles of right and justice, will not permit me to sanction this change.

These reasons for declining to give my consent to the bill, I submit with all deference for the consideration and judgment of your honorable body.

J.A. CAMPBELL

The Republicans in the House made an ineffectual effort to sustain the veto, but the party whip and the power of the saloons were too strong for them, and the bill was passed over the veto by a vote of 9 to 4. It met a different and better fate, however, in the Council, where it was sustained by a vote of 4 to 5.

How to Win the State Ballot

Abigail Scott Duniway

Abigail Scott Duniway started out her professional life as a schoolteacher and then as a woman's hatmaker. While working and interacting with women, she became aware of and concerned about the challenges that women faced. In 1871 she started and became the editor of the newspaper, *The New Northwest*. She invited prominent champions for women's rights, such as Susan B. Anthony and Elizabeth Cady Stanton, to come to Oregon to give speeches in favor of women's suffrage. When Anthony accepted her offer and held lectures throughout the Pacific Northwest, Duniway accompanied her, recorded their experiences, and sent these reports to be published in several newspapers, including her own.

Spurred on by the excitement of these engagements and becoming increasingly impassioned about the need for women to be able to vote, Abigail Scott Duniway became a champion for women's suffrage, playing a critical role in securing suffrage for women in the Washington Territory (1883), Washington State (1910), and Oregon (1912). She was even the first woman to cast a ballot in Oregon.

In this address from 1899, she shares her wisdom of fighting for female suffrage throughout the Northwest at the national conference of the National American Woman Suffrage Association (NAWSA), hoping to inspire the conference attendees as they carry on the fight in their respective states.

Excerpted from *Path Breaking: An Autobiographical History of the Equal Suffrage Movement in Pacific Coast States,* by Abigail Scott Duniway (New York: Source Book Press, 1970). Copyright © 1970 by Collectors Editions Ltd. Reprinted with permission.

Coming as I do from the far Pacific, where the sun at night sinks into the sea, to greet a convocation of co-workers from the far Atlantic, where the sun at morn rises out of the sea; and standing here, upon the central swell of the Middle West, where the sun at high noon kisses the heaving bosom of the mighty inland sea that answers back to East and West the echoing song of liberty, I realize the importance of my desire to speak to the entire continent, such tempered words as shall help to further unite our common interests in the great work that convenes us.

Work with Men, Not Against Them

The first fact to be considered, when working to win the ballot, is that there is but one way by which we may hope to obtain it, and that is by and through the affirmative votes of men. We may theorize, organize, appeal, argue, coax, cajole and threaten men till dooms-day; we may secure their pettings, praises, flattery, and every appearance of acquiescence in our demands; we may believe with all our hearts in the sincerity of their promises to vote as we dictate, but all of this will avail us nothing unless they deposit their affirmative votes in the ballot box.

Every man who stops to argue the case, as an opponent, tells us that he "loves women," and, while wondering much that he should consider such a declaration necessary, I have always admired the loyal spirit that prompts its utterance. But, gentlemen,—and I am proud indeed to see such a fine audience of you here tonight—there is another side to this expression of loyalty. Not only is our movement not instigated in a spirit of warfare between the sexes, but it is engendered, altogether, in the spirit of harmony, and interdependence between men and women, such as was the evident design of the great Creator when he placed fathers and mothers, brothers and sisters, in the same home and family. We are glad to be assured that you "love women," but we are doubly glad to be able, on proper occasions, and in every suitable way, to return the compliment. No good Equal Suffragist will any longer permit you to monopolize all the pretty speeches about the other sex. Every good woman in the world likes men a great deal better than she likes women, and there isn't a wise woman in all this goodly land who isn't proud to say so. We like you, gentlemen, and you cannot help it. We couldn't help it if we would; we wouldn't help it if we could. You like us, also, because you cannot help it. God made the sexes to match each other. Show me a woman who doesn't like men, and I will show you a sour-souled, vinegar-visaged specimen of unfortunate femininity, who owes the world an apology for living in it at all; and the very best thing she could do for her country, provided she had a country, would be to steal away and die, in the company of the man who doesn't like women. In order to gain the votes of men, so we can win the ballot, we must show them that we are inspired by the same patriotic motives that induce them to prize it. A home without a man in it, is only half a home. A government without women in it, is only half a government. Man without a woman is like one-half of a pair of dislocated shears. Woman without man is like the other half of the same disabled implement. Male and female created He them, saith the Higher Law, and to them God gave dominion "over every living thing upon the earth"—except each other.

Overcoming Men's Fears

Thirty years ago, when I began my humble efforts for securing the enfranchisement of women, away out upon the singing shores of the Pacific Sea, men everywhere imagined, at first, that the movement was intended to deprive them of a modicum of their liberties. They ought to have known this idea was absurd even then, as they have always had the power to both oppose or allow themselves to be ruled by women. But they thought legal supremacy over them was what women were after, and they met their own theory with hoarse guffaws of laughter. I had previously had much experience with the genus masculine, not only with my good husband, but with a large family of sons.

It is needless for me to tell you, after this confession, that

I am not young, and you can see for yourselves that I am no longer handsome.

The fact that men, for the most part, contented themselves in those early days of the Suffrage Movement, with exhibitions of ridicule, I accepted as a good omen. If you wish to convince a man that your opinion is logical and just, you have conquered the outer citadel of his resentment when he throws back his head and opens his mouth to laugh. Show me a solemn-visaged voter, with a face as long as the Pentateuch, and I will show you a man with a soul so little that it would have ample room to dance inside of a hollow mustard seed. Having tickled your opponent with a little nonsense, that at

Racism and Women's Suffrage

Many who campaigned for women's suffrage did so on the merits of giving women the right to vote. Unfortunately, others supported the cause merely as a way to offset the votes of African Americans, who were granted the right to vote with the Fifteenth Amendment. They thought that African American voters were ignorant and felt that giving white women the right to vote would help to dilute the impact of these African American voters. A southerner, Henry Blackwell, argues this point during a National American Woman Suffrage Association convention in Atlanta, Georgia, in 1895.

Apply it to your own State of Georgia, where there are 149,895 white women who can read and write, and 143,471 negro voters, of whom 116,516 are illiterates.

The time has come when this question should be considered. An educational qualification for suffrage may or may not be wise, but it is not necessarily unjust. If each voter governed only himself, his intelligence would concern himself alone, but his vote helps to govern everybody else. Society in conceding his right has itself a right to require from him a suitable preparation. Ability to read and write is absolutely necessary as a means of obtaining accurate political information. Without it the voter is almost sure to become the tool of political demagogues. With free schools

first was necessary to arrest his attention, you must then be careful to hold the ground you have gained. Your next step must be to impress upon all men the fact that we are not intending to interfere, in any way, with their rights; and all we ask is to be allowed to decide, for ourselves, also as to what our rights should be. They will then, very naturally, ask what effect our enfranchisement will have upon their politics. Visions of riotous scenes in political conventions will arise, to fill them with apprehension, as the possibility occurs that women, if enfranchised, will only double the vote and augment the uproar. They will recall partisan banquets, at which men have tarried over cups and pipes until they rolled under

provided by the States, every citizen can qualify himself without money and without price. Under such circumstances there is no infringement of rights in requiring an educational qualification as a pre-requisite of voting. Indeed, without this, suffrage is often little more than a name. "Suffrage is the authoritative exercise of rational choice in regard to principles, measures and men." The comparison of an unintelligent voter to a "trained monkey," who goes through the motion of dropping a paper ballot into a box, has in it an element of truth. Society, therefore, has a right to prescribe, in the admission of any new class of voters, such a qualification as every one can attain and as will enable the voter to cast an intelligent and responsible vote.

In the development of our complex political society we have today two great bodies of illiterate citizens: In the North, people of foreign birth; in the South, people of the African race and a considerable portion of the native white population. Against foreigners and negroes, as such, we would not discriminate. But in every State, save one, there are more educated women than all the illiterate voters, white and black, native and foreign.

Mari Jo Buhle and Paul Buhle, eds., *The Concise History of Woman Suffrage: Selections from the Classic Work of Stanton, Anthony, Gage, and Harper.* Urbana: University of Illinois Press, 1978, p. 337.

the table, or were carried off to bed on shutters. Very naturally, men, everywhere, object to seeing reputable women, and especially their own wives, engaged in such excesses. But our mighty men of the Pacific Northwest are troubled very little by these vagaries. They realize, as they sleep off the results of their latest political banquet, that at every public function in which their wives participate, there is a notable absence of any sort of dissipation. They remember that in former times, before good women had joined them, in the mining camps, mountain towns, and on the bachelor farms, that such scenes as sometimes transpire today, at men's great gatherings, were once so common as to excite little comment. It was the advent of good women in the border territories that changed all this, and eliminated the bad woman from social life, just as the ballot will eventually eliminate the bad woman from political life, where she now reigns supreme among men, having everything her own way. By the very charm of good women's presence they brought these changes about on the Pacific Coast, in social life, till men began to wonder how they had endured the old conditions, before the women joined them. Now, quite naturally, they are learning to apply this rule to politics; and so our men of the Pacific Coast are not alarmed, as many men are in other states, lest women, if allowed to become equal with themselves before the law, will forget their natural duties and natural womanliness. If, however, any man grows timid, and exhibits symptoms of alarm, as they sometimes do (even in Oregon), lest the balloted woman will forsake the kitchen sink, at which she has always been "protected" (without wages), or abandon the cooking stove, the rolling pin, the wash tub and the ironing board, at which she has always been shielded (without salary), we remind him that housekeeping and homemaking are, like everything else, undergoing a complete process of evolution. We show him that there is no more reason why every loaf of bread should be baked in a different kitchen than there is why every bushel of wheat should be ground in a different mill. We show him that the laundry is destined, hereafter, to keep pace with the threshing machine; the creamery with the spin-

while some of them were good people, well-educated, and came to stay, many were reckless, wicked and wandering. The first election was held in September, 1869, for the election of a delegate in congress, and members of the Council and House of Representatives for the first territorial legislature. There was a good deal of party feeling developed, and election day witnessed a sharp and vigorous struggle. The candidates and their friends spent money freely, and every liquor shop was thrown open to all who would drink. I was about to say that any one could imagine the consequences; but in fact I do not believe that any one could picture to himself the mad follies, and frightful scenes of that drunken election. Peaceful people did not dare to walk the streets, in some of the towns, during the latter part of the day and evening. At South Pass City, some drunken fellows with large knives and loaded revolvers swaggered around the polls, and swore that no negro should vote. One man remarked quietly that he thought the negroes had as good a right to vote as any of them had. He was immediately knocked down, jumped on, kicked and pounded without mercy, and would have been killed, had not his friends rushed into the brutal crowd and dragged him out, bloody and insensible. It was a long time before the poor fellow recovered from his injuries. There were quite a number of colored men who wanted to vote, but did not dare approach the polls until the United States Marshal placed himself at their head and with revolver in hand escorted them through the crowd, saying he would shoot the first man that interfered with them. There was much quarreling and tumult, but the negroes voted. This was only a sample of the day's doings, and characteristic of the election all over the territory. The result was that every Republican was defeated, and every Democratic candidate elected; and the whisky shops had shown themselves to be the ruling power in Wyoming. From such an inspiration one could hardly expect a revelation of much value! Yet there were some fair men among those elected.

The legislature met October 12, 1869. William H. Bright was elected president of the Council. As he was the author of the woman suffrage bill, and did more than all others to secure its passage, some account of him may be of interest. He was a man of much energy and of good natural endowments, but entirely without school education. He said frankly, "I have never been to school a day in my life, and where I learned to read and write I do not know." His character was not above reproach, but he had an excellent, well-informed wife, and he was a kind, indulgent husband.

ning jenny and power loom; the fruit cannery with the great flour mill; the dish washer with the steam-driven mangle, and the bakery with the ready-made clothing store.

Political Rights Will Yield Economic Rights

When women have been voters long enough to have acquired recognition of their own equal property rights with men, the servant girl problem will settle itself. When that time comes there will be no more work left to do in the home than the wife and mother can perform with comfort to herself and household; and the servant girls of today will then find systematic employment in the great factories, where food and clothing are manufactured by rule. This evolution has already begun with the woman typewriter. You see her everywhere; pretty, tidy, rosy with a ribbon or flower at her throat, intent upon her work and sure to get her pay. Then can the mother, for the sake of herself, her husband, and children, preserve her health, her beauty, and her mental vigor. Then can she be an adviser in the home, the state, the church, and the school, remaining so to a ripe old age.

But women can never have the opportunity, or the power, to achieve these results, except in isolated cases, till they are voters and lawmakers; and never even then, till they have had time to secure, by legislation, the equal property rights that they have earned with men from the beginning. . . .

Enfranchisement Will Not Jeopardize Men's Rights

But, your most important point, if you hope to win the ballot at all, is to convince the average voter, that, in seeking your liberties, you are equally anxious that he shall preserve his own. You may drive, or lead, a horse to water, but you cannot make him drink. Nor can you lead any man to vote for your enfranchisement till you have first convinced him that by so doing, he is not placing you in a position where you may, if you choose, trample upon any of his rights, whether they may be fancied or real, healthful or harmful. Every woman knows she cannot rule her husband. The man

who would be ruled by his wife would not be worth cor-
ralling in the chimney corner after she had driven him home.
What is true of men in the abstract, is equally true of men
in the aggregate. I cannot too strongly impress upon you,
good sisters, the fact that we will never get the ballot till the
crack of doom, if we persist in demanding it as a whip, with
which to scourge the real or apparent vices of the present
voting classes. If we can make men willing to be reformed,
they will then reform themselves.

Here is where woman has, in the last two decades, made
her greatest blunder. Whenever she demands the ballot, not
simply because it is her right to possess it, but because by
its use, she expects to reconstruct the genus man by law, on
a basis of her own choosing, she only succeeds in driving
nails into the closed coffin lid of her own and other women's
liberties.

Men know, intuitively, that the right to representation in
the legislature is a right as inestimable to us as to them; that
it is formidable to tyrants only. They do not believe themselves to be tyrants, and will resent the implication that they
are such to the bitter end. They also know that women, in
giving existence to the soldiers, suffer their full share of the
penalties and perils of existence, equaling all the horrors of
war. So, when they say, "Women must fight if they vote," it
is easy, in the awful glare of the tragedies of the present
year, to convince them in the words of Joaquin Miller, Oregon's greatest poet, that "The bravest battles that ever are
fought, are fought by the mothers of men.". . .

Again, we can never win the ballot by demanding it in the
interests of any particular "ism," union, party, sect or creed.
In our Pacific Northwest, the majority of the voters stand
ready to grant us the ballot whenever we demand it on the
broad basis of individual and collective liberty for ourselves;
and we will never get it otherwise.

Success in the Pacific Northwest

Our friends east of the Rocky Mountains were amazed and
electrified, in the autumn of 1883, by the announcement that

the Legislature of Washington Territory had extended the ballot to women.

Less than four years later, after a few self-imported agitators had made strong attempts to use the women's ballots for the enforcement of sumptuary legislation [concerning property rights], to which the men objected (even while pretending to approve it, till they got the women into a trap), women everywhere were dumfounded by the action of the politicians of the territory, who retaliated by shutting down the iron gates of a State Constitution in the women's faces, leaving them as ex-voters on the outside of the temple of liberty, with their hands tied.

The men of Washington are not yet over their scare, nor will they be till women have made an effort to convince them that the eyes of the great majority are now open, and they will never be entrapped in such a way again.

I pray you do not misunderstand me, friends. I wage no war upon any organization, or upon any person's political or religious faith. Catholics have just as good right to their religious opinions as Protestants. Republicans have just as good right to their political bias as Democrats, and Socialists have just as good a right to their reformatory fancies as Prohibitionists. Yet, if any one of these great armies of opposing opinions should claim Equal Suffrage as its chief dependence for success, and the great National American Woman Suffrage Association, or the Suffrage Association of any state, should become the champion of its special "ism," we should, henceforth, be unable to rally to our standard any appreciable vote, save that of the particular sect or party with which the voters of opposing sects or parties should believe us allied. We need all the votes we can get from all parties to win. . . .

The year 1900 is the period fixed by law for the final vote upon our pending Suffrage amendment, and we need have no fear for the result, if we can keep the fact before our voters that our demand for the ballot is not engendered by emotional insanity.

The men of our Pacific Northwest are a noble lot of free-

men. The spirit of enterprise which led them across the un-
tracked continent to form a new empire, beside our sundown
sea, was a bold and free spirit; and the patient heroism of
the few women who originally shared their lot had in it the
elements of grandeur.

There are lessons of liberty in the rockribbed mountains
that pierce our blue horizon with their snow-crowned heads,
and laugh to scorn the warring elements of the earth, the water and the air. There are lessons of freedom in our broad
prairies that roll away into illimitable distances. There are
lessons of equality in the gigantic, evenly-crested forest trees
that rear their hydra heads to the vaulted zenith and touch the
blue horizon with extended arms. There are lessons of truth
and justice in the very air we breathe, and lessons of irre-
sistible progress in the mighty waters that surge and sweep,
with superhuman power, between the overhanging bluffs of
our own Columbia, the "River of the West."

My state is the only one represented this year, in this great
Convention, in which an Equal Suffrage Amendment is
pending. The opportunity has come to us, as to the women
of no other state, to claim the dawn of the 20th century as
our year of jubilee. To work in unison with each other, and
with the women of the older states, crystallized with constitutions hoary with the encrustations of long-vanished
years, and compel them to look to the free, young, elastic
West, for the liberties they cannot get at home, is the proud
ambition that commands my presence here tonight. Help us
with your wisdom, your sympathy, your co-operation, good
friends; and when we shall have been successful at the ballot boxes of our state, thus adding a star of the first magnitude to the already bright constellation of our four free
states, which now illumine our Northwestern heavens, we
will entertain you with a national jubilee to celebrate our liberties, as the most fitting accompaniment to the dawn of the
20th century which patriotism can devise.

Campaigning Across a Dozen States

Anna Howard Shaw

Born in England, Anna Howard Shaw moved with her family to Michigan when she was four. She was the president of the National American Woman Suffrage Association (NAWSA) from 1904 to 1915. In an era when few women were allowed to become ministers or doctors, Anna Howard Shaw became both. She was ordained as a Methodist minister in 1880, and six years later she earned her M.D. from Boston University.

Her autobiography, *The Story of a Pioneer,* describes her life's work, with particular emphasis placed upon her role in the fight for women's suffrage. Part of her job as president of NAWSA was to go on lengthy speaking tours, in an attempt to convince various states to grant women the right to vote. As she explains in the following excerpt, this process took a long time. In 1912 she visited six separate states—Ohio, Michigan, Wisconsin, Oregon, Arizona, and Kansas—that were contemplating women's enfranchisement. Two years later, Shaw campaigned in the Dakotas, Montana, Nevada, Missouri, and Nebraska. Traveling to these states (and neighboring ones) provided Anna Howard Shaw with a wide array of experiences, from official receptions in Nebraska, hosted by the wife of the U.S. secretary of state, William Jennings Bryan, to a rodeo in Oregon.

The interval between the winning of Idaho and Utah in 1896 and that of Washington in 1910 seemed very long

Excerpted from *The Story of a Pioneer*, by Anna Howard Shaw with Elizabeth Jordan (New York: Harper and Brothers Publishers, 1915).

to lovers of the Cause. We were working as hard as ever—
harder, indeed, for the opposition against us was growing
stronger as our opponents realized what triumphant woman
suffrage would mean to the underworld, the grafters, and the
whited sepulchers [hypocrites] in public office. But in 1910
we were cheered by our Washington victory, followed the
next year by the winning of California. Then, with our
splendid banner year of 1912 came the winning of three
states—Arizona, Kansas, and Oregon—preceded by a campaign so full of vim and interest that it must have its brief
chronicle here.

Ohio, Michigan, Wisconsin, and Oregon

To begin, we conducted in 1912 the largest number of campaigns we had ever undertaken, working in six states in
which constitutional amendments were pending—Ohio,
Michigan, Wisconsin, Oregon, Arizona, and Kansas. Personally, I began my work in Ohio in August, with the modest aspiration of speaking in each of the principal towns in
every one of these states. In Michigan I had the invaluable assistance of Mrs. Lawrence Lewis, of Philadelphia, and I visited at this time the region of my old home, greatly changed
since the days of my girlhood, and talked to the old friends
and neighbors who had turned out in force to welcome me.
They showed their further interest in the most satisfactory
way, by carrying the amendment in their part of the state.

At least four and five speeches a day were expected, and
as usual we traveled in every sort of conveyance, from
freight-cars to eighty horse-power French automobiles. In
Eau Clair, Wisconsin, I spoke at the races immediately after the passing of a procession of cattle. At the end of the
procession rode a woman in an ox-cart, to represent pioneer
days. She wore a calico gown and a sunbonnet, and drove
her ox-team with genuine skill; and the last touch to the picture she made was furnished by the presence of a beautiful
biplane which whirred lightly in the air above her. The obvious comparison was too good to ignore, so I told my hear-
ers that their women today were still riding in ox-teams

while the men soared in the air, and that women's work in the world's service could be properly done only when they too were allowed to fly.

In Oregon we were joined by Miss Lucy Anthony. There, at Pendleton, I spoke during the great "round up," holding the meeting at night on the street, in which thousands of horsemen—cowboys, Indians, and ranchmen—were riding up and down, blowing horns, shouting, and singing. It seemed impossible to interest an audience under such conditions, but evidently the men liked variety, for when we began to speak they quieted down and closed around us until we had an audience that filled the streets in every direction and as far as our voices could reach. Never have we had more courteous or enthusiastic listeners than those wild and happy horsemen. Best of all, they not only cheered our sentiments, but they followed up their cheers with their votes. I spoke from an automobile, and when I had finished one of the cowboys rode close to me and asked for my New York address. "You will hear from me later," he said, when he had made a note of it. In time I received a great linen banner, on which he had made a superb pen-and-ink sketch of himself and his horse, and in every corner sketches of scenes in the different states where women voted, together with drawings of all the details of cowboy equipment. Over these were drawn the words: *Woman Suffrage—We are all for it.* The banner hangs to-day in the National Headquarters [of the National American Woman Suffrage Association].

Arizona and Kansas

In California Mr. Edwards presented me with the money to purchase the diamond in Miss Anthony's flag pin representing the victory of his state the preceding year; and in Arizona one of the highlights of the campaign was the splendid effort of Mrs. Frances Munds, the state president, and Mrs. Alice Park, of Palo Alto, California, who were carrying on the work in their headquarters with tremendous courage, and, as it seemed to me, almost unaided. Mrs. Park's specialty was the distribution of suffrage literature, which she circulated with remarkable judgment. The Governor of Arizona was in favor of our Cause, but there were so few active workers available that to me, at least, the winning of the state was a happy surprise.

In Kansas we stole some of the prestige of Champ Clark, who was making political speeches in the same region. At one station a brass-band and a great gathering were waiting for Mr. Clark's train just as our train drew in; so the local suffragists persuaded the band to play for us, too, and I made a speech to the inspiring accompaniment of "Hail to the Chief." The passengers on our train were greatly impressed, thinking it was all for us; the crowd at the station were glad to be amused until the great man came, and I was glad of the opportunity to talk to so many representative men—so we were all happy.

In the Soldiers' Home at Leavenworth I told the old men of the days when my father and brothers left us in the wilderness, and my mother and I cared for the home while they fought at the front—and I have always believed that much of the large vote we received at Leavenworth was cast by those old soldiers. . . .

The Dakotas, Montana, and Nevada

The campaign of 1914, in which we won Montana and Nevada, deserves special mention here. I must express also my regret that as this book will be on the presses before the campaign of 1915 is ended, I cannot include in these reminiscences the results of our work in New York and other states.

As a beginning of the 1914 campaign I spent a day in Chicago, on the way to South Dakota, to take my part in a moving-picture suffrage play. It was my first experience as an actress, and I found it a taxing one. As a modest beginning I was ordered to make a speech in thirty-three seconds— something of a task, as my usual time allowance for a speech is one hour. The manager assured me, however, that a speech of thirty-three seconds made twenty-seven feet of film— enough, he thought, to convert even a lieutenant-governor!

The Dakota campaigns, as usual, resolved themselves largely into feats of physical endurance, in which I was inspired by the fine example of the state presidents—Mrs. John Pyle of South Dakota and Mrs. Clara V. Darrow of North Dakota. Every day we made speeches from the rear platform of the trains on which we were traveling—sometimes only two or three, sometimes half a dozen. One day I rode one hundred miles in an automobile and spoke in five different towns. Another day I had to make a journey in a freight-car. It was, with a few exceptions, the roughest traveling I had yet known, and it took me six hours to reach my destination. While I

Anna Howard Shaw

was gathering up hair-pins and pulling myself together to leave the car at the end of the ride I asked the conductor how far we had traveled.

"Forty miles," said he, tersely.

"That means forty miles *ahead*," I murmured. "How far up and down?"

"Oh, a hundred miles up and down," grinned the conductor, and the exchange of persiflage [witty banter] cheered us both.

Though we did not win, I have very pleasant memories of North Dakota, for Mrs. Darrow accompanied me during the entire campaign, and took every burden from my shoulders so efficiently that I had nothing to do but make speeches.

In Montana our most interesting day was that of the State Fair, which ended with a suffrage parade that I was invited to lead. On this occasion the suffragists wished me to wear my cap and gown and my doctor's hood, but as I had not brought those garments with me, we borrowed and I proudly wore the cap and gown of the Unitarian minister. It was a small but really beautiful parade, and all the costumes for it were designed by the state president, Miss Jeannette Rankin, to whose fine work, by the way, combined with the work of her friends, the winning of Montana was largely due.

In Butte the big strike was on, and the town was under martial law. A large banquet was given us there, and when we drove up to the club-house where this festivity was to be held we were stopped by two armed guards who confronted us with stern faces and fixed bayonets. The situation seemed so absurd that I burst into happy laughter, and thus deeply offended the earnest young guards who were grasping the fixed bayonets. This sad memory was wiped out, however, by the interest of the banquet—a very delightful affair, attended by the mayor of Butte and other local dignitaries.

In Nevada the most interesting feature of the campaign was the splendid work of the women. In each of the little towns there was the same spirit of ceaseless activity and determination. The president of the State Association, Miss Anne Martin, who was at the head of the campaign work, accompanied me one Sunday when we drove seventy miles in a motor and spoke four times, and she was also my companion in a wonderful journey over the mountains. Miss Martin was a tireless and worthy leader of the fine workers in her state.

Missouri and Nebraska

In Missouri, under the direction of Mrs. Walter McNabb Miller, and in Nebraska, where Mrs. E. Draper Smith was managing the campaign, we had some inspiring meetings. At Lincoln [Nebraska] Mrs. William Jennings Bryan introduced me to the biggest audience of the year, and the programme took on a special interest from the fact that it included Mrs. Bryan's début as a speaker for suffrage. She is a tall and attractive woman with an extremely pleasant voice, and she made an admirable speech—clear, terse, and much to the point, putting herself on record as a strong supporter of the woman-suffrage movement. There was also an amusing aftermath of this occasion, which Secretary [of State] Bryan himself confided to me several months later when I met him in Atlantic City. He assured me, with the deep sincerity he assumes so well, that for five nights after my speech in Lincoln his wife had kept him awake listening to her report of it—and he added, solemnly, that he now knew it "by heart."

A less pleasing memory of Nebraska is that I lost my voice there and my activities were sadly interrupted. But I was taken to the home of Mr. and Mrs. Francis A. Brogan, of Omaha, and supplied with a trained nurse, a throat specialist, and such care and comfort that I really enjoyed the enforced rest—knowing, too, that the campaign committee was carrying on our work with great enthusiasm.

Lobbying the New York Senate

Harriot Stanton Blatch

Harriot Stanton Blatch was in many ways born to be a leader in the fight for women's suffrage. Her father, Henry Stanton, was active in the abolitionist movement. Her mother was Elizabeth Cady Stanton, a cofounder of the National Woman Suffrage Association.

In 1890, the National Woman Suffrage Association merged with Lucy Stone's American Woman Suffrage Association to form the National American Woman Suffrage Association (NAWSA). But the new organization was plagued with rivalries. Harriot Stanton Blatch grew restless of the internal politics so she formed her own group, the Equality League of Self-Supporting Women. In 1910, she changed her organization's name to the Women's Political Union (WPU). With the WPU, Blatch embarked on reinvigorating the suffrage movement with open-air meetings and a mass suffrage parade in New York City in 1910. She also believed that the fight for women's suffrage must also be taken to those who would eventually make the decision to grant women the right to vote: the state legislators. As this excerpt from her memoirs attests, Blatch led her organization in directly lobbying politicians—cajoling, browbeating, and charming legislators to pass the laws that would allow women the right to vote.

In the 1912 campaign to lobby state legislatures to embrace a women's suffrage bill, Blatch and her fellow suffragists were only partially successful. Their tactics were sufficient to force the New York Senate to move the suffrage bill from the

Excerpted from *Challenging Years: The Memoirs of Harriot Stanton Blatch*, by Harriot Stanton Blatch and Alma Lutz (New York: G.P. Putnam's Sons, 1940). Copyright © 1940 by G.P. Putnam's Sons. Reprinted with permission.

Judiciary Committee (where it had been languishing) to the Senate floor for formal debate. Unfortunately, despite Blatch's efforts, the opponents of women's suffrage used complicated legislative tactics to block the passage of the bill.

We had several friends on the Senate Judiciary Committee. The Chairman, Howard R. Bayne, who had been mildly interested in woman suffrage, had developed into a convinced and earnest advocate of our contention that the time had come when the Legislature had no right to hold back the question of the enfranchisement of women, and should pass it on to the voters for decision. Senator Burd and Senator Black were both tending to the same position. Senator Stilwell favored referring the question to the voters, solely, I believe, because he felt there should be fair play. He liked being credited with attachment to a respectable cause which did not offend big business interests with which he wished to be friendly. Senator Newcomb, alone, was a convinced suffragist, but he had never been trained by a group of suffragists who knew how to pull the wires of legislative procedure, to put punch into his convictions. . . .

Opponents of the Bill

While there was encouragement for us in the friendliness of these men, we had to face the fact that no Judiciary Committee had ever held for us such honest and able opponents. At the head of the enemy stood Harvey D. Hinman, perhaps the ablest man in the Senate at that time. He was a hardworking legislator. He always knew what was going on, and followed the intricate workings of the lawmaking machine intelligently and conscientiously. He was honest, strictly honest. I am sure he never wavered in his sound belief in democracy for the people. To his straightforward mind, women were not people. They were a kind of angel that must be protected by rugged man from contamination with the business and politics of a wicked world. . . . He brought passionate conviction and great ability to his exposition of the angel theory. I spent more thought on

Senator Hinman than on any other man in the Legislature, but he was immovable. . . .

Senator Ferris was another determined opponent and he knew quite as well as Hinman how to put the case of the angels. He was an able speaker, not as frank as Hinman for he walked more in line with the political machine. He fought for the angels right down to the time of the Syracuse Democratic Convention in October, 1912. He not only could not see when he was beaten, but could not grasp the magnitude of the force he was opposing. . . .

A Wink and a Smile

In other States, woman suffrage was making progress. In Wyoming, Colorado, Idaho, Utah, Washington, and California women were enfranchised. Oregon, Nevada, and Kansas had submitted the question to the voters. There had been favorable action in the Legislatures of five or six other states, and yet New York slept on. But we gave the legislators no peace.

Finally in desperation, the Women's Political Union inaugurated the "Silent Sentinels." Whenever the Judiciary Committees were in session, two of us stood at the door of the committee room, typifying the patient waiting that women had done since Elizabeth Cady Stanton made the first demand for our enfranchisement in 1848. While we had no immediate effect upon the committees, we did have on the press which gave us an immense amount of publicity.

Senator Bayne now suggested that we see for ourselves how hard he was working for action on the Suffrage bill and invited Caroline Lexow, Alberta Hill, and myself to be present at one of the meetings of the Judiciary Committee. Thus quite innocently I became the center of one of the circles that wily Hinman, Ferris, and Wagner cut around Senator Bayne.

Soon after the opening of the meeting, Senator Bayne began to tell us how genuinely he tried to bring the question to a vote, but was "balked by the absence of members whom we had reported as favorable, and who would certainly be present." Then he added how, under his guidance, the resolution had been kept before one committee after another, and had been respectfully and sympathetically discussed. Unfortunately, at this point, Hinman winked at me. If there ever was a revealing wink, that was. It spoke volumes. It declared the chairman's words all bunk, that the committee, as I well knew, had given no proper attention to reporting the Suffrage resolution. My response to the wink was a smile.

Alas, the wink had not been seen by Bayne, as Hinman was close at his left, but my smile shone full upon him. He stopped in his praise of the good faith of the committee and challenged my right to take his estimate of the committee's work so lightly. I was in a dilemma. I either had to show Hinman as the doubter of the devotedness of the committee by his revelatory wink, or I had to allow Bayne to hold the mistaken idea that I took his defense of the committee as a laughing matter. I had to think quickly and make a decision on the spot. I balanced Bayne's likelihood of helping the cause of suffrage against Hinman's determination to defeat us at every turn. Quickly I assured Senator Bayne that nothing was farther from my thoughts than to take his remarks lightly, my smile meant only a "polite recognition of a wink given to me by Senator Hinman." Hinman led the laugh, the other members followed, and Bayne half glared at Hinman and half smiled at me. The incident was over and no heads or hearts were broken.

Escorting Senators to Committee

Senator Bayne continued to insist that it was our responsibility to see that members of the committee attended meetings called to consider the Suffrage bill. He drew attention to the fact that Senator Black was absent. At once I asked if he meant that it was our duty to go out and bring Senator Black to the committee. He declared that was his view of the matter. Thereupon we withdrew to carry out our mission.

In conference in the corridor we decided that Caroline and Alberta were to unearth the hiding place of Senator Black and start the chase, and that I, the least athletic of the three, would take a position commanding a view of the committee door, the elevator, and the stairs, so that I might see where their startled hare took to cover.

They soon returned to me with the great news that they had seen him in the corridor above, but he had seen them and jumped into an elevator. Then came my news, "Yes, and got out at this floor and, without seeing me, sprinted to the office of the majority leader of the Senate, where he is at this very moment confiding, no doubt, to Senator Wagner his perilous predicament." It was obvious we must get in there with no announcement. We all knew the lay of the land—the large outer room occupied by the office force, and then the door in a distant corner leading to Wagner's sanctum. We had decided at our hasty confab that we must not allow ourselves to be announced, that we must steer our own entrance. So with an off-hand statement to the clerks that we had been sent by Senator Bayne to see Senator Black, we crossed to the door and gave a deferential rap, a bit heavy as if coming from masculine knuckles. In response, came Wagner's voice with an off-hand, "Come in." Quickly we opened the door upon two amazed faces.

"We are here, Senator Black," I declared, "at Senator Bayne's request to escort you to the Judiciary Committee."

One despairing look he gave Wagner. He expected aid. I could have told him he would get none. Wagner never aided a man in a mess, even though he had helped to make the path slippery. His motto seemed to be that politicians must "watch their steps" themselves.

Getting not the slightest sign from Wagner, Senator Black rose, and with me on his right and Alberta Hill on his left, and Caroline Lexow in a strategic position behind him, was escorted to the Judiciary Committee. On the short journey to the committee room, he remarked bitterly, "I'll never forgive this." And I retorted, "Oh, yes you will. Some day you will be declaring with pride how your vote advanced the Suffrage resolution." And thus did the Suffrage bill reach the Senate for consideration.

At the critical moment when the Senate seemed about to adjourn without action on our bill, the Women's Political

Union organized a deputation to Senator Wagner, the President pro tem of the Senate. We had suggested to the Legislative Cooperative Committee that all the Suffrage organizations join in carrying a great delegation to Albany on a special train. . . . On March 12, [we] took three hundred suffragists to the Capitol. Every window of the special train bore large placards reading, "If there is no good to be gained by a vote, why are men enfranchised?"; "The feeders of mankind want the vote to help lower the cost of food"; "We need the vote to protect our children"; "More ballots, less bullets." The entire delegation marched from the Albany station to the Capitol, almost every woman carrying a banner, a flag, or a placard of protest. . . .

Some fifty or sixty of us crowded into the committee room, the rest gathered in the corridor outside. There was but one door and that was on the corridor. The table and chair for the Senator were diagonally across in the farthest corner. The windows minus fire escapes opened on a court three stories below. Should our host, all unsuspecting venture into our trap, he would find himself at a great disadvantage from the start.

As the Senator passed down the wide, hospitable aisle from the door to the table and chair, the aisle space filled up just behind him solidly with delegates and even more delegates from the corridor. As he turned to face us he saw a determined mass of women, a little pale, wearing the tall fashionable headgear of the day, high-crowned, topped with waving plumes. We looked like grenadiers!

It was not long before he realized his situation. He was absolutely alone without a secretary, without even a telephone at his elbow. He quickly explained that he assigned this particular room, not knowing the delegation would be large. Most courteously he suggested we adjourn to the Senate Chamber where we would have seats. We thanked him for the kindness of the offer but declined as we were sure the business we had in hand would be quickly transacted. All we sought was an agreement on a date when the Senate could have full opportunity to debate and have a recorded vote on the Suffrage bill. It was then made quite clear by several speakers that his tactics were understood by the delegation, and that the issue covered by their bill was backed by a constituency covering the entire state and merited just handling by the majority leader. . . .

Like all other men in the Legislature, the Senator knew that when the Union planned pressure on a member, no inkling of the scheme was ever given out to the public. The unspoken agreement was always carefully adhered to: "Yield and there will be no publicity." Senator Wagner yielded, and the press wires did not carry a story about the Democratic majority leader of the New York Senate being held prisoner by three hundred irate suffragists. . . . He acceded to our request that facilities be given to the bill on March 19.

When the bill came up in the Senate on that day, so many men had been pledged in its favor that it needed the whole power of the opposition to defeat the measure. Senator Wagner used his great influence against us.

The Senate Debates

In the debate in the Senate, sitting as the Committee of the Whole with Senator Griffin in the chair, the opening speech was made by Senator Stilwell, the introducer of the bill. It was a clear, straightforward argument. Senator McClelland followed and dropped into biology and prenatal influences. He assured the Senators that the great handicap to the female sex is motherhood. "There is not a student today upon that subject," he declared, "that does not tell you that there are prenatal conditions that will affect the progeny. Men are not that way. If it had not been for the prenatal history, Napoleon would have been the greatest man in his time: but it is known that for four or five years before his birth, his mother followed the army in Corsica in fighting France. It was under these surroundings she gave to Napoleon his savage nature. . . . Had Napoleon's mother not been under that stress, he would have been born a blessing to mankind.". . . He added, "I want to repeat that I have been told that the fine function of woman is motherhood. It is well enough to say they do not get married, they have not got families. That does not make any difference. Motherhood is the true mission of womanhood today in this country.". . .

We sat without indulging a laugh, scarcely a smile, while the Senator nearly wept over the surcharged emotional nature of woman, her pre-ordained lack of self-control. As he closed, he referred to the fact that thirty years before, when in the Assembly he had voted in favor of woman suffrage.

Senator Timothy D. Sullivan deftly injected, "You had sense then."

Soon after the interruption, Big Tim was on his feet in regular order declaring he had been in the Legislature twenty-six years, and began by being for woman suffrage, and had seen no reason since to change his opinion. . . . He stated he was "out in Los Angeles the day of the last election and the ladies went up to the booth without any fuss and cast their ballot. The day is past now of scrambling at the polls and pulling and mauling. Any lady could go if she had the franchise, and cast a vote without any interference. And I don't think woman will turn out any less intelligent when she has the vote than now when she is not a voter.". . .

That very interesting character, Senator Hinman of Binghamton, took the line that the woman confined to the home was more valuable to society and her own family than a woman "chasing to the polls to vote on this, that, or the other question." He feared the disruptive effect in the home of political discussion. "It is all well enough for women to be interested in public questions so far as those that affect more or less the community and home, but let her devote her attention to the inculcation in her children of the duties of citizenship, teaching morality, and making the home what it should be. Feeling as I do, I believe I would be doing myself an injustice if I should vote to advance this legislation."

Senator Bayne's admirable speech was decidedly weakened by his opening explanation that he spoke because "in a moment of weakness he had pledged himself to do so to a charming woman.". . .

And so the verbal sparring among the Senators continued

until there came into play a clever use of the technicalities of procedure.

Senator Ferris from Utica, stated frankly that he was opposed to the initiative. He did believe, however, that if there were any general demand for woman suffrage, it probably ought to be referred to the people. As he had discovered no great demand, he therefore declared his opposition to the advancement of the bill.

Senator Stilwell, like a flash, asked "How are you going to vote on my motion?" He had been reminded by us that Senator Newcomb before going to Texas, had assured us he was paired[1] with Ferris.

Senator Ferris then entered into a lengthy explanation of how Senator Newcomb had come to him and told him that as a business trip would keep him from the Senate on March 19, it would be a great accommodation if he would pair with him on this vote. He had replied that if the Senate permitted, he would not vote, that he would be recorded against and Newcomb for the Suffrage resolution.

Then Senator Allen, who was opposed to advancing the Suffrage bill, made a request that another opponent, Senator Brackett who was at that time "engaged in argument in the Court of Appeals," should be recorded against advancing the bill, in case he were unable to get to the Senate Chamber to vote.

Unanimous consent was required. To Senator Wagner's declaration as majority leader, "No objection," and the chairman's, "Is there any objection?" Senator Bayne pluckily rose and declared, "I will make no objection only on condition that a similar request for others who are absent and cannot vote should be granted."

That meant a check-mate for our enemy, but Senator Wagner, a supreme political chess-player, was quickly on

---

1. "Pairing" is a legislative procedure in which one legislator in favor of a bill is put together with another who is opposed to the bill. If one member of the pair is unable to vote, his or her partner simply does not vote. Therefore, the outcome of the vote is the same, but pairing frees members of the legislature to attend to other business without worrying that their presence could have changed the final vote.

his feet commanding: "Then I ask the Senator (Allen) to withdraw his request, and I shall object to the Senator from the 36th (Ferris of Utica) being paired with the Senator from the 19th (Newcomb)."

Senator Wagner had been dashing up and down the Senate aisles, his goal being mainly Senator Ferris' seat. The whole maneuver was clear as crystal. Senator Brackett, arguing in the Court of Appeals, which in 1912 was housed in the Capitol and of course very accessible to the Senate Chamber, could perhaps pant through his thesis, rush and record his vote, while Ferris would be seemingly free to put in his body blow, as his pair champed at the bit in far-away Texas. There was a chance of getting Brackett's vote, and certainty of Ferris' if the pair were broken.

At this point, Senator Ferris pleaded, "May I ask the Senator from the 23rd (Bayne) if he will not permit Senator Brackett's name and vote to be counted in order that I may be excused from the disagreeable duty of voting in the absence of Senator Newcomb. I must vote if the Senate does not excuse me. It does not make any difference to the result."

Senator Bayne declared, "Of course I would not embarrass the gentleman in any way I could possibly avoid; but I think he is mistaken in assuring me he must vote. Nobody is obliged to vote. Our vote is only taken viva voce [i.e., a voice vote]."

Then practical Senator Wagner came to the rescue of the opposition by asking for a vote on his motion to strike out the enacting clause of the resolution. Stilwell then asked for a rising vote. Ferris broke his pair with Newcomb and the result was 21 to 17. We were out-maneuvered by only a few votes.

Why Massachusetts Voted Against Women's Suffrage

Ernest Bernbaum

The women's suffrage movement was not always successful in lobbying state legislatures. In 1915, Massachusetts put the idea of giving women the right to vote directly to the electorate. The end result was an overwhelming rejection of the referendum. Sixty-four and a half percent of those who participated voted against the provision. A Harvard professor of literature and frequent vocal opponent of granting women the right to vote was invited to write the introduction to a collection of essays "commemorating" the defeat of women's suffrage in Massachusetts. In his essay, Professor Ernest Bernbaum describes why he believes the push for female enfranchisement was unsuccessful. First, he argues that men were swayed by the fact that most women were cool to the idea of voting. Second, he suggests that such indifference would not allow the addition of women voters to improve the quality of politics as women suffragists often maintained. Finally, he characterizes the campaigning efforts of the suffragists as untruthful, strident, and unseemly, thereby undermining their cause.

The essays in this little book are by anti-suffrage women who were prominent speakers, writers, and organizers, in the campaign of 1915. They voice sentiments which gained the largest measure of popular support ever accorded

Excerpted from "Introduction," by Ernest Bernbaum in *Anti-Suffrage Essays*, by Massachusetts Women (Boston, MA: The Forum Publications of Boston, 1916).

in the history of Massachusetts politics.

The largest number of votes any political party polled in Massachusetts before 1915 was 278,976. The anti-suffragists polled 295,939. Since 1896 there has been but one instance in which the voters gained a plurality amounting to 110,000 votes. The anti-suffragists won by 133,447 votes. Alton B. Parker's defeat by Theodore Roosevelt in 1904 is commonly regarded as typifying political annihilation; but the suffragists in 1915 did not poll as many votes as Mr. Parker, and the anti-suffragists polled 38,000 more than President Roosevelt at the height of his popularity. Such outworn words as "overwhelming" and "landslide," which have been regularly used to describe victories not half so great as this, understate the actual extent of the anti-suffrage triumph. . . .

The grounds of this aversion are so numerous that it is difficult to determine which of the many causes of the anti-suffrage victory were the most powerful. In my opinion, however, Massachusetts men defeated woman suffrage chiefly because (1) they discovered that nine women out of ten did not want to vote; (2) they knew that the creation of a large body of stay-at-home voters would result in bad government; and (3) they grew disgusted with the temperament, the notions, and the methods typical of the few women who clamored for the vote.

No Interest in Voting

For at least two generations suffragists have been spending a huge amount of energy and money in spreading their doctrine. Contributions, mainly drawn from a few rich women, have enabled them to send professional speakers into every district of the state, to distribute tons of "literature," to supply the press with a constant stream of "news" written from their point of view, and in general to advertise their claims in the most lavish way. A propaganda so subsidized would have been successful decades ago if sound principles and common sense were on its side. But to their consternation the suffragists found that the vast majority of Massachusetts women turned a deaf ear to their plausible appeals, and that

During their campaigns, suffragists faced contempt and opposition from many men and women.

their strongest opponents were those of their own sex.

Suffragists continued to talk about what "we women" want. But men presently began to see that these women had no right to pretend to represent their sex. Even their own claims as to the number of women supporting them showed that they represented only between 5% and 10% of the women of Massachusetts. At least 90% of the women—either by open opposition, or by a marked indifference to the subject—showed that they did not believe in woman suffrage. It became obvious that no general statement could be more emphatically true than that Massachusetts women did not want to vote.

When this truth was insistently pressed upon the suffragists, they were apt to call the indifferent women "unenlightened." This was felt to be an insult rather than an explanation. The average Massachusetts man does not think his mother, wife, and sister "unenlightened"—certainly not on the suffrage question. She has heard and read the suffrage notions again and again. He knows that if she felt that man was her oppressor, or that the welfare of herself or her family would be increased by her enfranchisement, she would say so. She is a sensible, observant woman, who knows what she wants, does not hesitate to ask for it, and usually gets it. But she was not asking for the ballot. It did not take her long to see through the suffrage fallacy that "only those women would need to vote who want to." She realized that the vote would mean an obligation as well as a privilege, and that she could not honorably accept the privilege without undertaking the obligation. Her life being already crowded with duties that only she could discharge, she would not add to them one that her husband, brother, or son can discharge at least as well.

If any man wondered whether his personal inquiries among the women of his acquaintance gave a sufficiently broad basis for the belief that women did not want to vote, he became convinced of the fact when he learned about the Drury bill of 1913. This bill would have given Massachusetts women a chance to vote "Yes" or "No" on woman suffrage. The proposal resulted in the amazing revelation that the suffragists were afraid to let women vote on the question. They worked against the bill because they knew that an official count would disclose how pitiably small a fraction of women were on their side. They thought that their little group, by noisy publicity, could be made to appear a considerable number. But the men, when they discovered who opposed the Drury bill, were not deceived. They saw that a small minority of women was trying to induce them to coerce the great majority. They awoke to the fact that the suffragist's demand was not that men should grant women an expressed desire, but that men, contemptuously disregarding the evident wishes of women, should force upon them a heavy responsibility.

Lack of Interest in Politics

The nature of that responsibility brings us to what seems to me the second important cause for the suffrage defeat.

Men—more than politically inexperienced women—know that good government depends upon the willingness of the electorate to do its duty vigilantly and regularly. The greatest good of the greatest number of classes (including the women and children in each class) can be secured only when a large proportion of the eligible voters vote. Those voters who are led by bosses, or by selfish interests, go to the polls steadily. Their influence can be offset only when the rest of the electorate goes likewise. The results of elections in which a small proportion of the eligible voters take part, are poor laws and incompetent or corrupt government. The leading political issues—the tariff, trusts, transportation, military and police force, taxation, finance, etc.—bear directly upon the work of men in their trades and business, and under male suffrage a fairly large proportion of the vote is cast. The life-work of women removes them from contact with these political questions, and the nature of most women is not attracted by the contentious spirit in which political warfare is conducted. As long as no more than 10% of the women took an interest in the woman suffrage question itself, no man could reasonably expect them to be otherwise than indifferent to the regular subjects of political conflict. To impose political duties upon the sex against its will was simply to create conditions that encouraged corrupt and feeble government. The soundness of this principle was, furthermore, being demonstrated in woman-suffrage territory, such cities as Seattle and such states as Colorado showing that sooner or later a neglectful electorate leads to the downfall of good government.

Unethical Suffragists

The third cause for the defeat of woman suffrage was the disgust which the manners, methods, and unethical sentiments of the suffragists aroused. This is not pleasant to dwell upon, but was too important an influence in the campaign to leave unmentioned. The suffragists professed to "occupy higher moral ground," to uplift politics, and to elevate womanhood. The longer one observed their deeds and words, the surer one became that they were not uplifting politics and that they tended to disgrace women in men's eyes. The tone of politics can be improved if the contestants will avoid false assertions and unnecessary personal attacks. The suffragists said and did things which were, like militancy, excusable only on the immoral ground that the end justifies the means.

As an example of their disingenuous statements, the following may serve. The National Woman Suffrage Association circulated a flyer entitled "Twenty Facts About Woman Suffrage." "Fact No. 15," under the heading, "How Women Vote," read: "Arizona, California, Colorado and Washington are the only states in the Union which have eight-hour laws for working women." Any unsuspecting reader would infer just what he was intended to infer—namely, that it was woman suffrage that brought about all these eight-hour laws, and that male suffrage had not brought about any of them. A more nearly truthful heading for this "fact" would have been "How Men Vote." The credit for passing the eight-hour law in California and in Washington (also in Arizona so far as laundry workers are concerned) belongs to legislatures elected by men alone. False suggestions of this type no doubt gained many proselytes in parlor meetings; but when they were made in the open forum of a public campaign, their untruth was exposed, and the voters grew indignant that women should thus have tried to mislead them. The suffragists only made a bad matter worse by alleging that their anti-suffrage sisters were given to misrepresentations and to every other crime in the political calendar; for men thereupon concluded that if this initial participation in politics had such a demoralizing effect on the women of each side, it was best to keep both parties out of the arena altogether.

The suffragists' tendencies to make bitter personal attacks was repeatedly shown. Not wishing to resurrect some of the venemous charges brought against anti-suffrage women, I take leave to illustrate the baseless characters of such attacks by one made against myself. In the spring of 1915, I gave a series of lectures on the fundamental principles of anti-suffrage. The audiences were gratifyingly large; there was a demand for several repetitions of the lectures; and, apparently, the suffragists felt that something must be done to destroy my pernicious influence. Instead of answering my arguments, the President of the Massachusetts Suffrage Association, Miss Alice Stone Blackwell, wrote an editorial in her "Woman's Journal," saying:

"This young gentleman is a Dane, and he has been very fluent and somewhat contemptuous in giving reasons why American women should not be allowed to vote."

The statement was, as usual, spread broadcast through the suffrage columns of the Massachusetts newspapers; and doubtless my opponents indulged the hope that in the wave of national feeling which was then beginning to rise, anybody thus branded as a foreigner would be badly discredited. As a matter of fact, I was born in Brooklyn, N.Y. (If I had chosen to imitate Miss Blackwell's method of controversy, I might have retorted that my father, who was born in Denmark, but who came to America in 1855, fought as a volunteer officer in the Navy of the United States in the Civil War, at a time when Miss Blackwell's father was engaged in a safer occupation.)

The repellant impression made upon men by the suffragists' misstatements and personal abusiveness was deepened by their support of militancy and feminism. . . .

The greatest injury [militant suffragists] . . . did was to lower man's ideal of woman. They tried to make the virago a heroine. They did not succeed; . . . men were determined not to endorse a party that tempted women to abandon womanliness for mock masculinity.

Chapter 4

The Nineteenth Amendment

Chapter Preface

The women's suffrage movement, from its inception, faced a critical barrier to its goal of gaining the right to vote for all women. To be successful, women needed to convince legislators to change the current laws. But since women did not have the right to vote, they lacked an important means of influencing these legislators. If a legislator promised to vote in favor of women's suffrage and then later reneged, women could not punish that legislator by voting him out of office. Furthermore, the legislators had little incentive to grant voting rights to women. Once women got the right to vote, how could a legislator be certain that the newly enfranchised women would not exercise their right to vote for another candidate? Given these possible disadvantages, it is difficult to immediately understand why so many politicians eventually did vote in favor of the Anthony amendment, the name that was given to the Nineteenth Amendment that granted women's suffrage.

One reason that has been suggested is that, by 1914, enough states had given women the right to vote that the women's suffrage movement could actively press for a national solution. Some more militant suffragists felt that the increasing number of states that had women's suffrage could be used as an active political weapon to threaten those legislators who did not work actively to pass the federal amendment. Thus, in 1916, the National Woman's Party went to the states where women had the right to vote and campaigned against Woodrow Wilson and other Democratic candidates because the Democratic Party had not worked actively enough to propose the Anthony amendment. Members of the National American Woman Suffrage Association, however, distanced themselves from such a confrontational approach because they did not want to antagonize politicians, many of whom might be needed later if the two-thirds majority in the House and Senate needed to propose an amendment was to be achieved. Nevertheless, the fact that an increasing number of states had an electorate that included women spurred all suffrage organizations to focus their resources toward the passage and ratification of a constitutional amendment giving women the right to vote.

Another factor influencing politicians was America's entry into World War I. President Woodrow Wilson had kept the United States out of the war for as long as possible. Once it became clear that the United States could no longer stay out of the conflict, President Wilson justified U.S. involvement largely on the argument that it was helping to protect democracy across the world. However, supporters of women's suffrage argued that the fact that nearly half of the American population did not have the right to vote challenged the president's moral authority as a valiant protector of democracy. Thus, in 1918, after six years of only tepid support for women's suffrage, President Wilson took the unprecedented step of going to Congress to convince it to vote for a constitutional amendment that would give women the right to vote.

Such motivation, however, did not necessarily influence members of the House and Senate. While President Wilson worried about his image on the world stage, the members of Congress worried about pleasing the local voters who would determine whether they would be reelected. For politicians in states where women had the right to vote, supporters of women's suffrage threatened to mobilize women to vote against those politicians who did not support the constitutional amendment. Even politicians living in states where women did not enjoy the right to vote still felt pressure. The women's suffrage movement pointed out that there were important political gains that could be reaped by being seen as a champion for women's enfranchisement. If women got the right to vote and a legislator voted in favor of the amendment, then that politician could appeal to these new voters to strengthen his margin of victory in the next election.

All politicians felt some sort of political pressure in the debate over women's suffrage. The National American Woman Suffrage Association had become extremely effective in utilizing sophisticated lobbying tactics designed to bully, cajole, and otherwise convince reticent politicians to support their cause. All of these influential factors finally came together in 1919 when the House of Representatives and then the Senate proposed the Nineteenth Amendment and the state assemblies eventually ratified it.

The Winning Plan

Carrie Chapman Catt

National American Woman Suffrage Association president
Carrie Chapman Catt became frustrated when the suffrage
movement began to fragment. Some suffragists, like Alice
Paul, advocated a confrontational approach with politicians
and electorates. Others believed that direct confrontation with
the people who would be ultimately responsible for passing
and ratifying the longed-for constitutional amendment
seemed counterproductive. Furthermore, the various state-
level organizations had not done a good job of coordinating
their efforts with each other or with the national organization.

At the 1916 annual convention, Carrie Chapman Catt presented to the Executive Council (which included the national
officers and the president of each state branch) what eventually became known as her "Winning Plan." This plan, which
remained officially secret, required the state suffrage associations to pledge themselves to her six-year strategy, which sys-
tematically described what pressure would be needed to get
two-thirds of Congress to propose and three-fourths of the
state legislatures to ratify the Nineteenth Amendment.

W hen thirty-six state associations, or preferably more,
enter into a solemn compact to get the [Federal]
Amendment submitted by Congress and ratified by their respective legislatures; when they live up to their compact by
running a red-hot, never-ceasing campaign in their own
states designed to create sentiment behind the political leaders of the states and to aim both these forces at the men in

Excerpted from Carrie Chapman Catt's speech before the National American Woman Suffrage Association convention, 1916.

Congress as well as the legislatures, we *can* get the Amendment through, and ratified. We cannot do it by any other process. No such compact has ever been made, and no virile intention exists in the minds of the majority of the Association to back up a Washington lobby. Whether this is due to a prevailing belief that a lobby, assisted now and then by a bombardment of letters and telegrams, can pull the Amendment through, or to a lack of confidence in suffrage by the Federal route, or to sheer, unthinking carelessness, I am not prepared to say. I am inclined to believe that all three of these causes exist. . . .

This Convention must not adjourn, should it sit until Christmas, until it creates a logical and sensible policy toward the Federal Amendment. . . . If it be decided that we *do* want enfranchisement by the Federal route, then at least thirty-six states must sign a compact to go after it with a will. . . .

National Boards must be selected hereafter for one chief qualification—the ability to lead the national fight. There should be a mobilization of at least thirty-six state armies, and these armies should move under the direction of the national officers. They should be disciplined and obedient to the national officers in all matters concerning the national campaign. This great army with its thirty-six, and let us hope, forty-eight divisions [reflecting the forty-eight states in the Union at the time], should move on Congress with precision, and a will. . . . More, those who enter on this task, should go prepared to give their lives and fortunes for success, and any pusillanimous coward among us who dares to call retreat, should be courtmartialled.

Any other policy than this is weak, inefficient, illogical, silly, inane, and ridiculous! Any other policy would fail of success. . . .

Needed Victories

When a general is about to make an attack upon the enemy at a fortified point, he often begins to feint elsewhere in order to draw off attention and forces. If we decide to train up some states into preparedness for campaign, the best help which can be given them is to keep so much "suffrage noise" going all over the country that neither the enemy nor friends will discover where the real battle is. . . .

We should win, if it is possible to do so, a few more states before the Federal Amendment gets up to the legislatures. . . . A southern state should be selected and made ready for a campaign, and the solid front of the "anti" south broken as soon as possible.

Some break in the solid "anti" East should be made too. If New York wins in 1917 the backbone of the opposition will be largely bent if not broken. . . .

By 1920, when the next national party platforms will be adopted, we should have won Iowa, South Dakota, North Dakota, Nebraska, New York, Maine and a southern state. We should have secured the Illinois law in a number of other states.

With these victories to our credit and the tremendous increase of momentum given the whole movement, we should be able to secure planks in all platforms favoring the Federal Amendment (if it has not passed before that time) and to secure its passage in the December term of the 1920 Congress.

It should then go to the legislatures of thirty-nine states which meet in 1921, and the remaining states would have the opportunity to ratify the amendment in 1922. If thirty-six states had ratified in these two years, the end of our struggle would come by April 1, 1922, six years hence. . . .

It will require, however, a constructive program of hard, aggressive work for six years, money to support it, and the cooperation of all suffragists. It will demand the elimination of the spirit of criticism, back-biting and narrow-minded clashing of personalities which is always common to a stagnant town, society or movement, and which is beginning to show itself in our midst. Success will depend less on the money we are able to command, than upon our combined ability to lift the campaign above this sordidness of mind, and to elevate it to the position of a crusade for human freedom.

Mobilizing Lobbyists to Pressure Congressmen

Maud Wood Park

In 1917, despite the tremendous progress the women's suffrage movement had made in gaining the right to vote for
women in several states, too many states had yet to consider
women's suffrage legislation. Even though a large proportion
of women still did not have the right to vote, Maud Wood
Park believed that the state-level elements of the National
American Woman Suffrage Association (NAWSA) could still
exert considerable influence on members of Congress before
these legislators came to Washington to decide on the issue.
However, such a strategy demanded a meticulous attention to
details. Maud Wood Park, as the chair of the Congressional
Committee of NAWSA, saw the coordination of these direct
lobbying efforts as her primary job. Taken from her 1960
memoir, Park's letter to state-level suffragists could serve as
useful advice for any interest group that hopes to get elected
officials to support their cause and pass legislation in favor of
their group's goals.

Then, just when it was hardest for me to give thought to
anything else,[1] the chairman of our Congressional Committee was obliged by family duties to resign, and I was ap-

1. The author refers to her concern over World War I, which the United States officially
entered in 1917.

pointed by the National Board to take her place. I dreaded the responsibility too much to accept it readily. First I tried to persuade Helen Gardener, whose extraordinary gifts I was beginning to appreciate, to be chairman. She refused because of her husband's failing health, though she promised to be vice-chairman. Then I told the Board I was not sufficiently familiar with Congressional procedure to direct the work. But that objection was removed by the Board's agreement to engage, as temporary adviser, Dr. Alexander J. McKelway, who had been the legislative representative of the Child Labor Committee when the first child labor bill passed the Congress. With the further assurance that Miss Ruth White, of Missouri, the able secretary of our committee since June, 1916, would continue in that office, I reluctantly accepted the appointment. . . .

In spite of our absorption in the possibility of war, we knew that we had to prepare for our campaign for the amendment in the Sixty-fifth Congress. So Ruth White and I wrote our letter of directions to state Congressional chairmen—a letter that I quote in full because it is explicit in regard to the help counted on and, in most cases, received from our state workers:

March 21, 1917

Dear Congressional Chairman:

The 65th Congress has been called together on April 2nd. Although we cannot tell what the extra session may bring forth, we hope that the need of political justice for women will be more apparent than ever before and that openings may arise which we had not foreseen. It is imperative that we should take advantage of every possibility in our favor. For that reason, there is urgent need for activity in the home districts of Members of Congress. Will you therefore please give immediate attention to the following requests.

I. Reports

There are several new members with regard to whom we have had no word from their own state. Please send us *immediately* a statement, as full as you are able to make it, about the men whose names are enclosed.

CAUTION. Although we are most anxious to know how the Members of Congress stand with regard to the Federal Amendment, we beg you to take the utmost care that no Member is allowed to commit himself *against* the Amendment when he can be prevented from doing so. If you think he is inclined to be opposed, let us know your opinion; but in your letters to him and in your interviews, frame your appeals in such a way that they will not offer opportunity for a negative answer.

II. DELEGATIONS

If time allows and unless you have already done this work, delegations should visit your new Members before they leave for Washington. Delegations should be sent also to the old Members who are reported as "non-committal" or "opposed." Old Members who are in favor should be seen less formally, thanked for their position in the past, and given to understand, in a friendly and cordial way, that we are confident of their continued support.

In this connection, we ought all to remind ourselves constantly that Members expect to be treated as individuals. Do not permit circular letters to be sent them; but in writing or visiting them, be sure to make clear that you differentiate the individual from the group. In the case of friendly men, great harm has been done by writing or speaking as if their previous records were unknown and their support unappreciated.

Care should be taken in forming delegations to choose, if possible, women whose families have political influence in the man's own party and who are representative of the different sections of his district. It is well to have a small group of persons of real importance in the District rather than a large group of less prominent people. Effective use should be made of our recent remarkable gains in Ohio, North Dakota, Indiana and Canada. For example, copies of the maps giving the increase of suffrage territory might be shown and a statement made of our gain in electoral votes.

Please let us know what you are able to do in this matter.

III. WORK BY MEN

INDIVIDUAL CALLS. The best advice that we have been able to get with regard to our work in the coming session bids us lay much more emphasis on *work by men in the home Districts*. We therefore urge you to try to get men of political prominence to call, apparently casually, on your Congressmen before they return to Washington to express to them the hope that they may support the Federal Amendment. The more men you can get to make these calls the better, for they will be enormously effective. They should be quite apart from the delegations.

COMMITTEES OF MEN. While you are seeking men to make these personal calls, it would be well also to start in each Congressional District a committee or group of men prominent in politics or in other ways who will agree to help as the need may arise by sending letters and telegrams to the Congressmen. When such a committee or group has been formed, a list of its members with addresses should be sent to our office with the name of the District Congressional Chairman through whom they can be reached. Mrs. [Carrie Chapman] Catt [NAWSA president] in her letter of March 12th wrote you in this connection. We are merely reminding you and urging you to make every effort to secure as many influential men as possible for these committees.

IV. COMPLETION OF STATE CONGRESSIONAL COMMITTEES

Mrs. Catt also urged you to complete your list of District Congressional Chairmen, if such list is not already filled. The Chairman of each District should make herself responsible for the accumulation of all information with regard to her Congressman which could possibly be of use to the workers in Washington. She should know about his political, social and personal standing, what influences effected his election, what pressure he would most quickly feel, his previous record in Congress and any earlier political record he may have. If he is a former member of the State Legislature, she should know what kind of bills he sponsored in the legislature and whether he is progressive or reactionary with regard to social and humanitarian measures. In short, she should know all about him, and most important of all, she should pass that information on to us in Washington in order that we may make the best possible use of it.

SPECIAL. In addition to your chairman for each Congressional District, you should appoint two members "at large" each of whom should hold herself responsible for one of your Senators in the same manner in which the Congressional District Chairman is responsible for the Representative from her District. Will you kindly send us the names of those two members-at-large as soon as possible?

V. STATE ORGANIZATION WORK

When your State is planning its organization work, can you not arrange with the State Organization Committee to put its full force into the Districts whose Representatives in Congress are on your "doubtful" list? It is possible that the reason why that Representative is "doubtful" is that the suffrage organization in his District is weak. If you could send an organizer into that District to stir up new suffrage sentiment or to make articulate and effective the feeling that is already there, the man might be swung into our ranks for the coming session. If you can accomplish this with even one of your "doubtful" men, you will have done much toward the end which we are all hoping to attain in this coming Congress. We look to the State Congressional Chairmen and their lieutenants in the Congressional District to make this hope an accomplished fact.

SUMMARY

We shall then expect from you:

I. An immediate report on the new members whose names are enclosed.

II. An early report of any delegations that you are able to arrange.

III. A list of members of your men's committees with their addresses.

IV. The names of the two members-at-large on your State Congressional Committee and the names of any District Chairmen who may have been appointed since your last report to us.

Your National Committee hopes to hear from you more frequently during the coming year. We are convinced that our fighting strength must lie chiefly in a connection with our state organizations represented by the State Congressional Chairmen. We urge you, therefore, to share with us freely all the wisdom which you may have. Your suggestions and criticism at any time, as well as your active co-operation, will be heartily appreciated.

Very cordially yours,

Maud Wood Park, Chairman
Ruth White, Secretary
NATIONAL CONGRESSIONAL COMMITTEE

Refuting Arguments Against Suffrage

Alice Stone Blackwell

In 1917, as part of their work in pressuring for a constitutional amendment granting women the right to vote, the National American Woman Suffrage Association (NAWSA) published a collection of pamphlets that had been written by their organization and by other famous proponents of women's suffrage. Alice Stone Blackwell, a prominent member of NAWSA, wrote one such pamphlet that was included in the collection. Her pamphlet is meant to provide advocates for female enfranchisement a comprehensive list of the primary objections that had been made to giving women the right to vote. Filled with clever and memorable anecdotes, Alice Stone Blackwell's pamphlet provides suffragists with responses to each of these objections to help them prepare for public speeches and debates in favor of women's suffrage.

Why Should Women Vote?

The reasons why women should vote are the same as the reasons why men should vote—the same as the reasons for having a republic rather than a monarchy. It is fair and right that the people who must obey the laws should have a voice in choosing the law-makers, and that those who must pay the taxes should have a voice as to the amount of the tax, and the way in which the money shall be spent.

Roughly stated, the fundamental principle of a republic

Excerpted from *"The Blue Book": Woman Suffrage—History, Arguments, and Results*, edited by Frances M. Björkman and Annie G. Porritt (New York: National Woman Suffrage Publishing Company, Inc., 1917).

is this: In deciding what is to be done, we take everybody's opinion, and then go according to the wish of the majority. As we cannot suit everybody, we do what will suit the greatest number. That seems to be, on the whole, the fairest way. A vote is simply a written expression of opinion.

In thus taking a vote to get at the wish of the majority, certain classes of persons are passed over, whose opinions for one reason or another are thought not to be worth counting. In most of our states, these classes are children, aliens, idiots, lunatics, criminals and women. There are good and obvious reasons for making all these exceptions but the last. Of course no account ought to be taken of the opinions of children, insane persons, or criminals. Is there any equally good reason why no account should be taken of the opinions of women? Let us consider the reasons commonly given, and see if they are sound.

Are Women Represented?

Women are represented already by their husbands, fathers and brothers.

This so-called representation bears no proportion to numbers. Here is a man who has a wife, widowed mother, four or five unmarried sisters, and half a dozen unmarried daughters. His vote represents himself and all these women, and it counts one; while the vote of his bachelor neighbor next door, without a female relative in the world, counts for just as much. Since the object of taking a vote is to get at the wish of the majority, it is clear that the only fair and accurate way is for each grown person to have one vote, and cast it to represent himself or herself.

American men are the best in the world, and if it were possible for any men to represent women, through kindness and good will to them, American men would do it. But a man is by nature too different from a woman to be able to represent her. The two creatures are unlike. Whatever his good will, he cannot fully put himself in a woman's place, and look at things exactly from her point of view. To say this is no more a reflection upon his mental or moral ability than it would be a reflection upon his musical ability to say that he cannot sing both soprano and bass. Unless men and women should ever become alike (which would be regrettable and monotonous), women must either go unrepresented or represent themselves. . . .

Is "Influence" Enough?

If the laws are unjust, they can be corrected by women's indirect influence.

Yes, but the indirect method is needlessly long and hard. If women were forbidden to use the direct route by rail across the continent and complained of the injustice, it would be no answer to tell them that it is possible to get from New York to San Francisco by going around Cape Horn. . . .

The Bad Women's Vote

The bad women would outvote the good ones.

In America, the bad women are so few, compared with the good ones, that their votes could have little influence. . . .

"The bad women represent, in any city of the United States, but an infinitesimal proportion of its population, and the vote of that class in Denver is confined practically to three precincts out of 120."

The late Mrs. Sarah Platt Decker, of Denver, at one time President of the General Federation of Women's Clubs and also of the Colorado State Board of Charities and Correction, wrote:

"Does not the vote of the disreputable class of women overbalance the better element? No; the women of the half-world are not willing to vote. They are constantly changing their residences and their names. They do not wish to give any data concerning themselves, their age, name or number of street; they prefer to remain unidentified."

Ex-Gov. Warren, of Wyoming, sums it all up when he says, in a letter to Horace G. Wadlin, of Massachusetts:

"Our women nearly all vote; and since, in Wyoming as elsewhere, the majority of women are good and not bad, the result is good and not evil."

Don't Understand Business

A municipality is a great business corporation. Men, by the nature of their occupations, know more about business than women, and hence are better fitted to run a city or a state.

Women have a vote in every other corporation in which they are shareholders. George William Curtis said: "A woman may vote as a stockholder upon a railroad from one end of the country to the other; but, if she sells her stock and buys a house with the money, she has no voice in the laying out of the road before her door, which her house is taxed to keep and pay for."

Moreover, it is not true that a man's experience in his own business teaches him how to carry on the business of a city. Some years ago, a fashionable caterer was elected to the Massachusetts Legislature, and was appointed a member of the committee on filling up the South Boston flats. Another member said to him scornfully, "What do you know about filling up flats, anyway?" The caterer answered quietly, "That has been my business for twenty years." The answer was good, as a joke; but as a matter of fact, what had his experience of planning dinners taught him about the way to turn tide-mud into solid ground? What does the butcher learn from his business about the best way to pave a street, or the baker about the best way to build a sewer, or the candle-stick maker about the best way to lay out a park, or to choose school teachers or policemen, or to run a city hospital? Does a minister learn from his profession how to keep the streets clean, or a lawyer how to conduct a public school, or a doctor how to put out a fire? A man's business, at best, gives him special knowledge only in regard to one or two departments of city affairs. Women's business, as mothers and housekeepers, also gives them special knowledge in regard to some important department of public work, those relating to children, schools, playgrounds, the protection of the weak and young, morals, the care of the poor, etc. For what lies outside the scope of their own experience, men and women alike must rely upon experts. All they need, as voters, is sense enough and conscience enough to elect honest and capable persons to have charge of these things. . . .

Would Lose Their Influence

Women would lose their influence.

What gives a woman influence? Beauty, goodness, tact, talent, pleasant manners, money, social position, etc. A woman who has any of these means of influence now would still have them if she had a vote and she would have this other potent means of influence besides. There is a story of a prisoner who had been shut up for many years in a dungeon, getting sunlight only through a chink in the wall. He grew much attached to that chink. At last his friends came and offered to tear down the wall. His mind had become weakened and he begged them not to do it. If they destroyed the wall, he said, they would also destroy the chink through which he got his sunlight, and he would be left in total darkness. If he had had his wits he would have seen that he would have all the sunlight he had before, and a great deal more besides. A woman after enfranchisement would have all the personal influence she has now, and political influence in addition. One thing is certain. Every vicious interest in this country, to which women are hostile, would rather continue to contend with women's "indirect influence" than try to cope with women's vote. . . .

Already Overburdened

Women are already overburdened. A woman would not have time to perform her political duties without neglecting higher duties.

Mrs. Alice Freeman Palmer wrote:

"How much time must she spend on her political duties? If she belongs to the well-to-do-class, and hires others to do her work, she has time for whatever interests her most— only let these interests be noble! If she does her own housework, she can take ten minutes to stop on her way to market and vote once or twice a year. She can find half an hour a day for the newspapers and other means of information.

She can talk with family and friends about what she reads. She does this now; she will then do it more intelligently and will give and receive more from what she says and hears. If she does this reading and talking, she will be better informed than the majority of voters are now. The duties of motherhood and the making of a home are the most sacred work of women and the dearest to them, of every class. If casting an intelligent vote would interfere with what only women can do—and what, failed in, undermines society and government—no one can question which a woman must choose. But it cannot be shown that there are any large number of women in this country who have not the necessary time to vote intelligently, and it can be argued that study of

Women's Suffrage as a Commodity

Historian Margaret Finnegan argues that American suffragists found it personally and politically useful to link their demands for voting rights to the growing consumerism of the day. While often an expedient technique, this strategy also limited the scope of reform to voting rights rather than a broader set of economic and social rights for women.

Whatever the social ill, suffragists identified votes for women as the remedy.

This logic contained a consumeristic streak. As [political and social critic] Frederic Jameson notes, consumer capitalistic societies demonstrate the remarkable ability to redefine abstract principles and ideals as tangible things. Suffragists did so by making the right to vote synonymous with physical possession of a ballot. They then recast the ballot as a household appliance—something neatly stocked in any housewife's pantry. By the 1900s, suffragists had begun comparing the ballot to vacuums, telephones, and sewing machines. Like these items, it was a handy household helper. A suffrage leaflet printed by the New York Woman Suffrage Party concluded that the ballot and the sewing machine both acted as "labor-saving machine[s] for the home." Just as women with sewing machines could sew more quickly than

the vital questions of our government would make them better comrades to their husbands and friends, better guides to their sons, and more interesting and valuable members of society. Women of every class have more leisure than men, are less tied to hours of routine; they have had more years of school training than men. All this makes simple the combination of public and higher duties.". . . .

Doubling the Vote

It would only double the vote without changing the result.

If letting women sing in church merely doubled the volume of sound, it would still be a good thing, because it would double the number of persons who had the lung ex-

---

those without, so women with the vote could quickly—and literally—"clean up the city." And as the clearly ridiculous remarks of the puckish character Mad Hatter in the play *A Suffrage Rummage Sale* indicate, denying women suffrage was like denying housewives vacuums—adding to women's daily grind by making them "go on toiling and moiling—scrubbing and sweeping—in the good old-fashioned way."

Expediency arguments also transformed the ballot into a form of political currency. One illustrated suffrage flyer (most likely from the 1910s) showed "the vote" hanging like dollar bills out of a woman's purse as she listened to two politicians hawking "proposed legislation for the home." "Rival candidates for office are competitors for the woman's vote just as much as rival grocers are for her patronage," noted the flyer. . . .

In effect, politicians became merchants, legislation became a commodity, and women voters became comparison shoppers. Given this construction of government and citizenship, it is not surprising that supporters of women's enfranchisement went to the one place where women had best honed their shopping skills: the department store.

Margaret Finnegan, *Selling Suffrage: Consumer Culture and Votes for Women.* New York: Columbia University Press, 1999, p. 27.

ercise and the inspiration of joining in a good hymn and it would make the chorus stronger. If equal suffrage merely doubled the number of votes it would still do good, because to take an interest in public affairs would give women mental stimulus and greater breadth of view; and it would also bring to bear on public problems the minds of an increased number of intelligent and patriotic citizens. But the great advantage of women in music is that they add the soprano and alto to the tenor and bass. If women were exactly like men, equal suffrage would merely double the vote. But women are different from men; and women's voices in the State, like women's voices in the choir, would be the introduction of a new element. This is recognized even by opponents, when they express the fear that equal suffrage would lead to "sentimental legislation."

Men are superior to women along certain lines, and women superior to men along certain others. The points of weakness in American politics at present are precisely the points where women are strong. There is no lack in our politics of business ability, executive talent, or "smartness" of any kind. There is a dangerous lack of conscience and humanity. The business interests, which appeal more especially to men, are well and shrewdly looked after; the moral and humanitarian interests, which appeal more especially to women, are apt to be neglected. . . .

Too Many Voters

We have too many voters already.

This only means that we have too many voters of the wrong kind. If to increase the number of voters were an evil in itself, every woman who becomes the mother of half a dozen sons would have done harm to her country. But if all six grow up to be good voters she has conferred a benefit on her country. So she has, if five of them become good voters, and only one a bad voter. Woman suffrage would bring in at least five good voters to one bad one.

It is often said that we have too many immigrants. We mean too many immigrants of an undesirable kind. We all rejoice when we hear of a large influx from Finland or some other country whose people are considered especially desirable immigrants. We want them to offset those of less virtuous and law-abiding races. The governor of one of the enfranchised States writes of woman suffrage: "The effect of this increase in the vote is the same as if a large and eminently respectable class of citizens had immigrated here."

Would Unsex Women

It will turn women into men.

The differences between men and women are natural; they are not the result of disfranchisement. The fact that all men have equal rights before the law does not wipe out natural differences of character and temperament between man and man. Why should it wipe out the natural differences between men and women? The women of England, Scotland, Canada, Yucatan, Ireland, Australia, New Zealand, the Scandinavian countries and our own equal suffrage States are not perceptibly different in looks or manners from women elsewhere, although they have been voting for years. . . .

Women Do Not Want It

Whenever the majority of women ask for suffrage, they will get it.

Every improvement in the condition of women thus far has been secured not by a general demand from the majority of women, but by the arguments, entreaties and "continual coming" of a persistent few. In each case the advocates of progress have had to contend not merely with the conservatism of men, but with the indifference of women, and often with active opposition from some of them.

When a man in Saco, Me., first employed a saleswoman, the men boycotted his store, and the women remonstrated with him on the sin of placing a young woman in a position of such "publicity." When Lucy Stone began to try to secure for married women the right to their own property, women asked with scorn, "Do you think I would give myself where I would not give my property?" When Elizabeth Blackwell began to study medicine, women at her boarding house refused to speak to her, and women passing her on the street held their skirts aside. It is a matter of history with what ridicule and opposition Mary Lyon's first efforts for the higher education of women were received, not only by the mass of men, but by the mass of women as well. . . .

All this merely shows that human nature is conservative, and that it is fully as conservative in women as in men. The persons who take a strong interest in any reform are generally few, whether among men or women, and they are habitually regarded with disfavor, even by those whom the proposed reform is to benefit.

Many changes for the better have been made during the last half century in the laws, written and unwritten, relating to women. Everybody approves of these changes now, because they have become accomplished facts. But not one of them would have been made to this day if it had been necessary to wait till the majority of women asked for it. The change now under discussion is to be judged on its merits. In the light of history the indifference of most women and the opposition of a few must be taken as a matter of course. It has no more rational significance now than it has had in regard to each previous step of women's progress.

Jailed for Protesting

Doris Stevens

Some women's groups believed that direct action needed to be taken if women were ever going to get the right to vote. One such group was Alice Paul's National Woman's Party (NWP), which had split from the more mainstream National American Woman Suffrage Association (NAWSA), particularly because Paul felt that NAWSA had become too complacent and conservative in its goals and tactics. Instead she created the NWP to instigate more direct action, such as her campaign to protest in front of the White House.

The picketing began in January 1917. At first President Wilson was generally amused by these protests. His temperament changed after the United States officially entered World War I in April 1917. He asked women to stop their picketing as a show of solidarity and support for the war effort. NAWSA agreed, but NWP did not, suggesting that their cause was more just than ever since Wilson had argued that America's involvement in the war was necessary to secure democracy throughout the world. President Wilson ordered the protesters to be arrested. In all, a total of 218 women were arrested and given sentences ranging from three days to seven months.

The conditions faced by the prisoners, who were held primarily at the Occoquan workhouse in Virginia, were deplorable, including worms in the food, long days of arduous work, and even physical beatings. Doris Stevens, a social worker, observed them firsthand when she was arrested and sentenced to sixty days in the workhouse. President Wilson pardoned her three days later, but while incarcerated, Stevens observed and experienced how terribly the women were being

Excerpted from *Jailed for Freedom*, by Doris Stevens (Freeport, NY: Books for Libraries Press, 1920).

treated, simply because they were fighting for what they believed was right. Combining her observations with those of other women who were arrested for picketing the White House, Stevens wrote a book, *Jailed for Freedom,* which was published in 1920. This excerpt is taken from that book.

D uring all this time the suffrage prisoners were endur- ing the miserable and petty tyranny of the government workhouse at Occoquan. They were kept absolutely incommunicado. They were not allowed to see even their nearest relatives, should any be within reach, until they had been in the institution two weeks.

Each prisoner was allowed to write one outgoing letter a month, which, after being read by the warden, could be sent or withheld at his whim.

All incoming mail and telegrams were also censored by the Superintendent and practically all of them denied the prisoners. Superintendent Whittaker openly boasted of holding up the suffragists' mail: "I am boss down here," he said to visitors who asked to see the prisoners, or to send in a note. "I consider the letters and telegrams these prisoners get are treasonable. They cannot have them." He referred to messages commending the women for choosing prison to silence, and bidding them stand steadfast to their program.

Of course all this was done in the hope of intimidating not only the prisoners, but also those who came wanting to see them.

It was the intention of the women to abide as far as possible by the routine of the institution, disagreeable and unreasonable as it was. They performed the tasks assigned to them. They ate the prison food without protest. They wore the coarse prison clothes. But at the end of the first week of detention they became so weak from the shockingly bad food that they began to wonder if they could endure such a system. The petty tyrannies they could endure. But the inevitable result of a diet of sour bread, half-cooked vegetables, rancid soup with worms in it, was serious.

Documenting the Horrible Conditions

Finally the true condition of affairs trickled to the outside world through the devious routes of prison messengers.

Senator J. Hamilton Lewis, of Illinois, Democratic whip in the Senate, heard alarming reports of two of his constituents, Miss Lucy Ewing, daughter of Judge Ewing, niece of Adlai Stevenson, Vice-President in Cleveland's Administration, niece of James Ewing, minister to Belgium in the same Administration, and Mrs. William Upton Watson of Chicago. He made a hurried trip to the workhouse to see them. The fastidious Senator was shocked—shocked at the appearance of the prisoners, shocked at the tale they told, shocked that "ladies" should be subjected to such indignities. "In all my years of criminal practice," said the Senator to Gilson Gardner, who had accompanied him to the workhouse, "I have never seen prisoners so badly treated, either before or after conviction." He is a gallant gentleman who would be expected to be uncomfortable when he actually saw ladies suffer. It was more than gallantry in this instance, however, for he spoke in frank condemnation of the whole "shame and outrage" of the thing.

It is possible that he reported to other Administration officials what he had learned during his visit to the workhouse for very soon afterwards it was announced that an investigation of conditions in the workhouse would be held. That was, of course, an admirable manœuvre which the Administration could make. "Is the President not a kind man? He pardoned some women. Now he investigates the conditions under which others are imprisoned. Even though they are lawless women, he wishes them well treated."

It would sound "noble" to thousands.

Immediately the District Commissioners announced this investigation, Miss Lucy Burns, acting on behalf of the National Woman's Party, sent a letter to Commissioner Brownlow. After summing up the food situation Miss Burns wrote:

> When our friends were sent to prison, they expected the food would be extremely plain, but they also expected that . . . enough

eatable food would be given them to maintain them in their ordinary state of health. This has not been the case.

The testimony of one of the prisoners, Miss Lavinia Dock, a trained nurse, is extremely valuable on the question of food supplied at Occoquan. Miss Dock is Secretary of the American Federation of Nurses. She has had a distinguished career in her profession. She assisted in the work after the Johnstown flood and during the yellow fever epidemic in Florida. During the Spanish war she organized the Red Cross work with Clara Barton. 'I really thought,' said Miss Dock, when I last saw her, 'that I could eat everything, but here I have hard work choking down enough food to keep the life in me.'

I am sure you will agree with me that these conditions should be instantly remedied. When these and other prisoners were sentenced to prison they were sentenced to detention and not to starvation or semi-starvation.

The hygienic conditions have been improved at Occoquan since a group of suffragists were imprisoned there. But they are still bad. The water they drink is kept in an open pail, from which it is ladled into a drinking cup. The prisoners frequently dip the drinking cup directly into the pail.

The same piece of soap is used for every prisoner. As the prisoners in Occoquan are sometimes seriously afflicted with disease, this practice is appallingly negligent.

Concerning the general conditions of the person, I am enclosing with this letter, affidavit of Mrs. Virginia Bovee, an ex-officer of the workhouse. . . . The prisoners for whom I am counsel are aware that cruel practices go on at Occoquan. On one occasion they heard Superintendent Whittaker kicking a woman in the next room. They heard Whittaker's voice, the sound of blows, and the woman's cries.

I lay these facts before you with the knowledge that you will be glad to have the fullest possible information given you concerning the institution for whose administration you as Commissioner of the District of Columbia are responsible.

Very respectfully yours,

(Signed) Lucy Burns.

A Prison Employee Speaks Out

Mrs. Bovee, a matron, was discharged from the workhouse because she tried to be kind to the suffrage prisoners. She also gave them warnings to guide them past the possible contamination of hideous diseases. As soon as she was discharged from the workhouse she went to the headquarters of the Woman's Party and volunteered to make an affidavit. The affidavit of Mrs. Bovee follows:

I was discharged yesterday as an officer of Occoquan workhouse. For eight months I acted as night officer, with no complaint as to my performance of my duties. Yesterday Superintendent Whittaker told me I was discharged and gave me two hours in which to get out. I demanded the charges from the matron, Mrs. Herndon, and I was told that it was owing to something that Senator Lewis has said.

I am well acquainted with the conditions at Occoquan. I have had charge of all the suffragist prisoners who have been there. I know that their mail has been withheld from them. Mrs. Herndon, the matron, reads the mail, and often discussed it with us at the officers' table. She said of a letter sent to one of the suffragist pickets now in the workhouse, "They told her to keep her eyes open and notice everything. She will never get that letter," said Mrs. Herndon. Then she corrected herself, and added, "Not until she goes away." Ordinarily the mail not given the prisoners is destroyed. The mail for the suffragists is saved for them until they are ready to go away. I have seen three of the women have one letter each, but that is all. The three were Mrs. Watson, Miss Ewing, and I think Miss Flanagan.

The blankets now being used in the prison have been in use since December without being washed or cleaned. Blankets are washed once a year. Officers are warned not to touch any of the bedding. The one officer who handles it is compelled by the regulations to wear rubber gloves while she does so. The sheets for the ordinary prisoners are not changed completely, even when one is gone and another takes her bed. Instead the top sheet is put on the bottom, and one fresh sheet is given them. I was not there when these suffragists arrived, and I do not know how their bedding was arranged. I doubt whether the authorities would have dared to give them one soiled sheet.

The prisoners with disease are not always isolated, by any means. . . . Women suffering from syphilis, who have open sores, are put in the hospital. But those whose sores are temporarily healed are put in the same dormitory with the others. There have been several such in my dormitory.

When the prisoners come they must undress and take a shower bath. For this they take a piece of soap from a bucket in the store room. When they are finished they throw the soap back in the bucket. The suffragists are permitted three showers a week and have only these pieces of soap which are common to all inmates. There is no soap at all in wash rooms.

The beans, hominy, rice, cornmeal (which is exceedingly coarse, like chicken feed) and cereal have all had worms in them. Sometimes the worms float on top of the soup. Often they are found in the cornbread. The first suffragists sent the worms to Whittaker on a spoon. On the farm is a fine herd of Holsteins. The cream is made into butter and sold to the tuberculosis hospital in Washington. At the officers' table we have very good milk. The prisoners do not have any butter or sugar, and no milk except by order of the doctor.

Prisoners are punished by being put on bread or water, or by being beaten. I know of one girl who has been kept seventeen days on only water this month in the "booby house." The same was kept nineteen days on water last year because she beat Superintendent Whittaker when he tried to beat her.

Superintendent Whittaker or his son are the only ones who beat the girls. Officers are not allowed to lay a hand on them in punishment. I know of one girl beaten until the blood had to be scrubbed from her clothing and from the floor of the "booby house." I have never actually seen a girl beaten, but I have seen her afterwards and I have heard the cries and blows. Dorothy Warfield was beaten and the suffragists heard the beating.

(Signed) MRS. VIRGINIA BOVEE.

Subscribed and sworn to before
me this day of August, 1917.
JOSEPH H. BATT, *Notary Public.*

While the Administration was planning an investigation of the conditions in the workhouse, which made it difficult for women to sustain health through a thirty day sentence, it was, through its police court, sentencing more women to *sixty day sentences*, under the same conditions. The Administration was giving some thought to its plan of procedure, but not enough to master the simple fact that women would not stop going to prison until something had been done which promised passage of the [women's suffrage] amendment through Congress.

Punishment, Intimidation, and Humiliation

New forms of intimidation and hardship were offered by Superintendent Whittaker.

Mrs. Frederick Kendall of Buffalo, New York, a frail and highly sensitive woman, was put in a "punishment cell" on bread and water, under a charge of "impudence." Mrs. Kendall says that her impudence consisted of "protesting to the matron that scrubbing floors on my hands and knees was too severe work for me as I had been unable for days to eat the prison food. My impudence further consisted in asking for lighter work."

Mrs. Kendall was refused the clean clothing she should have had the day she was put in solitary confinement and was thus forced to wear the same clothing eleven days. She was refused a nightdress or clean linen for the cot. Her only toilet accommodations was an open pail. For four days she was allowed no water for toilet purposes. Her diet consisted of three thin slices of bread and three cups of water, carried to her in a paper cup which frequently leaked out half the meagre supply before it got to Mrs. Kendall's cell.

Representative and Mrs. Charles Bennet Smith, of Buffalo, friends of Mrs. Kendall, created a considerable disturbance when they learned of this cruel treatment, with the result that Mrs. Kendall was finally given clean clothing and taken from her confinement. When she walked from her cell to greet Mrs. Genevieve Clark Thompson, daughter of Champ Clark, Speaker of the House, and Miss Roberta Bradshaw, other friends, who, through the Speaker's influence, had obtained special permission to see Mrs. Kendall, she fell in a dead faint. It was such shocking facts as these that the Commissioners and their investigating board were vainly trying to keep from the country for the sake of the reputation of the Administration.

For attempting to speak to Mrs. Kendall through her cell door, to inquire as to her health, while in solitary, Miss Lucy

Burns was placed on a bread and water diet.

Miss Jeannette Rankin of Montana, the only woman member of Congress, was moved by these and similar revelations to introduce a resolution calling for a Congressional investigation of the workhouse. . . .

Solidarity and Singing Among the Prisoners

Charming companionships grew up in prison. Ingenuity at lifting the dull monotony of imprisonment brought to light many talents for camaraderie which amused not only the suffrage prisoners but the "regulars." Locked in separate cells, as in the District Jail, the suffragists could still communicate by song. The following lively doggerel to the tune of "Captain Kidd" was sung in chorus to the accompaniment of a hair comb. It became a saga. Each day a new verse was added, relating the day's particular controversy with the prison authorities.

> We worried Woody-wood,[1]
> As we stood, as we stood,
> We worried Woody-wood,
> As we stood.
> We worried Woody-wood,
> And we worried him right good;
> We worried him right good as we stood.
>
> We asked him for the vote,
> As we stood, as we stood,
> We asked him for the vote
> As we stood,
> We asked him for the vote,
> But he'd rather write a note,
> He'd rather write a note—so we stood.
>
> We'll not get out on bail,
> Go to jail, go to jail—
> We'll not get out on bail,
> We prefer to go to jail,
> We prefer to go to jail—we're not frail.

1. Refers to President Woodrow Wilson

We asked them for a brush,
For our teeth, for our teeth,
We asked them for a brush,
For our teeth.
We asked them for a brush,
They said, "There ain't no rush,"
They said, "There ain't no rush—darn your teeth."

We asked them for some air,
As we choked, as we choked,
We asked them for some air
As we choked.
We asked them for some air
And they threw us in a lair,
They threw us in a lair, so we choked.

We asked them for our nightie,
As we froze, as we froze,
We asked them for our nightie
As we froze.
We asked them for our nightie,
And they looked—hightie-tightie—
They looked hightie-tightie—so we froze.

Now, ladies, take the hint,
As ye stand, as ye stand,
Now, ladies, take the hint,
As ye stand.
Now, ladies, take the hint,
Don't quote the Presidint,
Don't quote the Presidint, as ye stand.

Humor predominated in the poems that came out of prison. There was never any word of tragedy.

Not even an intolerable diet of raw salt pork, which by actual count of Miss Margaret Fotheringham, a teacher of Domestic Science and Dietetics, was served the suffragists *sixteen times in eighteen days*, could break their spirit of gaiety. And when a piece of fish of unknown origin was slipped through the tiny opening in the cell door, and a specimen carefully preserved for Dr. Wiley—who, by the way, was unable to classify it—they were more diverted than outraged. . . .

Again prisoners would build a song, each calling out from cell to cell, and contributing a line. The following song to the tune of "Charlie Is My Darling" was so written and sung: . . .

SHOUT THE REVOLUTION OF WOMEN

Shout the revolution
   Of women, of women,
Shout the revolution
   For liberty.
Rise, glorious women of the earth,
   The voiceless and the free
United strength assures the birth
   Of true democracy.

REFRAIN

Invincible our army,
   Forward, forward,
Triumphant daughters pressing
   To victory.

Shout the revolution
   Of women, of women,
Shout the revolution
   For liberty.
Men's revolution born in blood,
   But ours conceived in peace,
We hold a banner for a sword,
   Till all oppression cease.

REFRAIN

Prison, death, defying,
   Onward, onward,
Triumphant daughters pressing
   To victory.

The gaiety was interspersed with sadness when the suffragists learned of new cruelties heaped upon the helpless ones, those who were without influence or friends. They learned of that barbarous punishment known as "the greasy pole" used upon girl prisoners. This method of punishment consisted of strapping girls with their hands tied behind them to a greasy pole from which they were partly suspended. Unable to keep themselves in an upright position, because of the grease on the pole, they slipped almost to the floor, with their arms all but severed from the arm sockets, suffering intense pain for long periods of time. This cruel punishment was meted out to prisoners for slight infractions of the prison rules.

The suffrage prisoners learned also of the race hatred which the authorities encouraged. It was not infrequent that the jail officers summoned black girls to attack white women, if the latter disobeyed. This happened in one instance to the suffrage prisoners who were protesting against the warden's forcibly taking a suffragist from the workhouse without telling her or her comrades whither she was being taken. Black girls were called and commanded to physically attack the suffragists. The [black prisoners], reluctant to do so, were goaded to deliver blows upon the women by the warden's threats of punishment.

The President Appeals to the Senate

Woodrow Wilson

According to the U.S. Constitution, amending the document requires a two-thirds majority in both houses of Congress before it can be sent to the states for their ratification. In this address to the Senate on September 10, 1918, President Woodrow Wilson hoped to persuade wavering senators to pass the Nineteenth Amendment to the Constitution, which would grant women the right to vote. Although Wilson had previously seemed hesitant to deliver on his promises to suffragists, this address was meant to signal the renewed importance that he placed on giving women the legal right to vote throughout the United States.

APPEAL OF PRESIDENT WILSON TO THE SENATE OF THE UNITED STATES TO SUBMIT THE FEDERAL AMENDMENT FOR WOMAN SUFFRAGE DELIVERED IN PERSON SEPT. 30, 1918.

Gentlemen of the Senate: The unusual circumstances of a World War in which we stand and are judged in the view not only of our own people and our own consciences but also in the view of all nations and peoples, will, I hope, justify in your thought, as it does in mine, the message I have come to bring you.

I regard the concurrence of the Senate in the constitutional amendment proposing the extension of the suffrage to women as vitally essential to the successful prosecution

Excerpted from *The History of Woman Suffrage*, vol. 5, edited by Ida Husted Harper (New York: J.J. Little and Ives Company, 1922).

of the great war of humanity in which we are engaged. I have come to urge upon you the considerations which have led me to that conclusion. It is not only my privilege, it is also my duty to apprise you of every circumstance and element involved in this momentous struggle which seems to me to affect its very processes and its outcome. It is my duty to win the war and to ask you to remove every obstacle that stands in the way of winning it.

I had assumed that the Senate would concur in the amendment, because no disputable principle is involved but only a question of the method by which the suffrage is to be now extended to women. There is and can be no party issue involved in it. Both of our great national parties are pledged, explicitly pledged, to equality of suffrage for the women of the country.

Neither party, therefore, it seems to me, can justify hesitation as to the method of obtaining it, can rightfully hesitate to substitute Federal initiative for State initiative if the early adoption of this measure is necessary to the successful prosecution of the war, and if the method of State action proposed in the party platforms of 1916 is impracticable within any reasonable length of time, if practical at all. And its adoption is, in my judgment, clearly necessary to the successful prosecution of the war and the successful realization of the objects for which the war is being fought.

That judgment I take the liberty of urging upon you with solemn earnestness for reasons which I shall state very frankly and which I shall hope will seem as conclusive to you as they seem to me.

This is a people's war and the people's thinking constitutes its atmosphere and morale, not the predilections of the drawing room or the political considerations of the caucus. If we be indeed democrats and wish to lead the world to democracy, we can ask other peoples to accept in proof of our sincerity and our ability to lead them whither they wish to be led, nothing less persuasive and convincing than our actions.

Our professions will not suffice. Verification must be forthcoming when verification is asked for. And in this case

By appealing to the Senate, Wilson helped to pass the Nineteenth Amendment that granted women's suffrage.

verification is asked for—asked for in this particular matter. You ask by whom? Not through diplomatic channels; not by foreign ministers; not by the intimations of parliaments. It is asked for by the anxious, expectant, suffering peoples with whom we are dealing and who are willing to put their destinies in some measure in our hands, if they are sure that we wish the same things that they do.

I do not speak by conjecture. It is not alone that the voices of statesmen and of newspapers reach me, and that the voices of foolish and intemperate agitators do not reach me at all. Through many, many channels I have been made aware what the plain, struggling, workaday folk are thinking, upon whom the chief terror and suffering of this tragic war fall. They are looking to the great, powerful, famous democracy of the West to lead them to the new day for which they have so long waited; and they think, in their logical simplicity, that democracy means that women shall play their part in affairs alongside men and upon an equal footing with them.

If we reject measures like this, in ignorant defiance of what a new age has brought forth, of what they have seen but we have not, they will cease to believe in us; they will cease to follow or to trust us. They have seen their own governments accept this interpretation of democracy—seen old governments like that of Great Britain, which did not profess to be democratic, promise readily and as of course this justice to women, though they had before refused it; the strange revelations of this war having made many things new and plain to governments as well as to peoples.

Are we alone to refuse to learn the lesson? Are we alone to ask and take the utmost that our women can give—service and sacrifice of every kind—and still say we do not see what title that gives them to stand by our side in the guidance of the affairs of their nation and ours? We have made partners of the women in this war. Shall we admit them only to a partnership of suffering and sacrifice and toil and not to a partnership of privilege and right? This war could not have been fought, either by the other nations engaged or by America, if it had not been for the services of the women—services rendered in every sphere—not merely in the fields of efforts in which we have been accustomed to see them work but wherever men have worked and upon the very skirts and edges of the battle itself.

We shall not only be distrusted, but shall deserve to be distrusted if we do not enfranchise women with the fullest possible enfranchisement, as it is now certain that the other great free nations will enfranchise them. We cannot isolate our thought or action in such a matter from the thought of the rest of the world. We must either conform or deliberately reject what they approve and resign the leadership of liberal minds to others.

The women of America are too intelligent and too devoted to be slackers whether you give or withhold this thing that is mere justice; but I know the magic it will work in their thoughts and spirits if you give it to them. I propose it as I would propose to admit soldiers to the suffrage—the men fighting in the field of our liberties of the world—were they excluded.

The tasks of the women lie at the very heart of the war and I know how much stronger that heart will beat if you do this just thing and show our women that you trust them as much as you in fact and of necessity depend upon them.

An Important Part of the War Effort

I have said that the passage of this amendment is a vitally necessary war measure and do you need further proof? Do you stand in need of the trust of other peoples and of the trust of our own women? Is that trust an asset or is it not? I tell you plainly, as the commander-in-chief of our armies and of the gallant men in our fleets; as the present spokesman of this people in our dealings with the men and women throughout the world who are now our partners; as the responsible head of a great government which stands and is questioned day by day as to its purpose, its principles, its hope. . . . I tell you plainly that this measure which I urge upon you is vital to the winning of the war and to the energies alike of preparation and of battle.

And not to the winning of the war only. It is vital to the right solution of the great problems which we must settle, and settle immediately, when the war is over. We shall need in our vision of affairs, as we have never needed them before, the sympathy and insight and clear moral instinct of the women of the world. The problems of that time will strike to the roots of many things that we have hitherto questioned, and I for one believe that our safety in those questioning days, as well as our comprehension of matters that touch society to the quick, will depend upon the direct and authoritative participation of women in our counsels. We shall need their moral sense to preserve what is right and fine and worthy in our system of life as well as to discover just what it is that ought to be purified and reformed. Without their counsellings we shall be only half wise.

That is my case. This is my appeal. Many may deny its validity, if they choose, but no one can brush aside or answer the arguments upon which it is based. The executive tasks of this war rest upon me. I ask that you lighten them and place in my hands instruments, spiritual instruments, which I have daily to apologize for not being able to employ.

Celebrating Victory and Looking Forward

National American Woman Suffrage Association

The fifty-first convention of the National American Woman Suffrage Association, held in Chicago in February 1920, was called the "Victory Convention" by the organization. Although the Nineteenth Amendment had not yet been ratified by three-fourths of the states, it seemed to the members of NAWSA that it was only a matter of time before women's suffrage would become part of the Constitution. Therefore, much of the time at the convention was dedicated to celebration and reflection over the many battles that had been fought in order to secure American women the right to vote.

At the same time, the movement knew that considerable work remained undone. Many leaders wanted to use the existing organization, with its grassroots support and other resources, to push for further rights for women. Therefore, with very little opposition, NAWSA agreed to dissolve itself once the Nineteenth Amendment was ratified since its primary objective, universal suffrage for all American women, would have been achieved. However, the convention also agreed to create a new organization, the League of Women Voters, designed primarily to educate and mobilize women to use their voting rights actively. This organization remains politically active to the present day. The following description of the NAWSA convention comes from the fifth volume of *The History of Woman Suffrage*, a compilation of suffrage writings.

Excerpted from *The History of Woman Suffrage*, vol. 5, edited by Ida Husted Harper (New York: J.J. Little and Ives Company, 1922).

The official report of the Fifty-first convention, in 1920, was entitled Victory Convention of the National American Woman Suffrage Association and First Congress of the League of Women Voters and the Call was as follows:

"Suffragists, hear this last call to a suffrage convention!

"The officers of the National American Woman Suffrage Association hereby call the State auxiliaries, through their elected delegates, to meet in annual convention at Chicago, Congress Hotel, February 12th to 18th, inclusive. In other days our members and friends have been summoned to annual conventions to disseminate the propaganda for their common cause, to cheer and encourage each other, to strengthen their organized influence, to counsel as to ways and means of insuring further progress. At this time they are called to rejoice that the struggle is over, the aim achieved and the women of the nation about to enter into the enjoyment of their hard-earned political liberty. Of all the conventions held within the past fifty-one years, this will prove the most momentous. Few people live to see the actual and final realization of hopes to which they have devoted their lives. That privilege is ours.

"Turning to the past let us review the incidents of our long struggle together before they are laid away with other buried memories. Let us honor our pioneers. Let us tell the world of the ever-buoyant hope, born of the assurance of the justice and inevitability of our cause, which has given our army of workers the unswerving courage and determination that at last have overcome every obstacle and attained their aim. Come and let us together express the joy which only those can feel who have suffered for a cause.

"Turning to the future, let us inquire together how best we can now serve our beloved nation. Let us ask what political parties want of us and we of them. Come one and all and unitedly make this last suffrage convention a glad memory to you, a heritage for your children and your children's children and a benefaction to our nation."

The seven days of the convention were divided between the National Association and the League of Women Voters,

the latter having the lion's share as a new organization requiring much time and attention. All of February 12 was
given to the meetings of its committees, with dinners for all
delegates and a program of speakers at the Auditorium,
Morrison and La Salle Hotels in the evening. . . .

Convention Attendance and Agenda

The convention of the National Association began February
13 but the two preceding days had been occupied by almost
continuous business sessions of the officers and board of directors. Mrs. Grace Wilbur Trout, [Illinois] State president,
was chairman of the local committee of arrangements of
nearly forty women of Chicago, Evanston and suburban
towns for this largest national suffrage convention ever held
and the arrangements had never been surpassed. Nothing was
forgotten which could contribute to the success or pleasure
of the convention. A hostess was appointed for each State to
make its delegates acquainted and contribute to their comfort. There were present 546 delegates, a large number of al-
ternates and thousands of visitors, while for the audience at
the public meetings there was not even standing room.

At the morning session on the 13th, with Mrs. [Carrie
Chapman] Catt presiding, the following program was presented by the Executive Council for the consideration of the
delegates and was discussed at this and other business sessions:

1. Shall the National American Woman Suffrage Association dissolve when the last task concerning the extension
of suffrage to women is completed?

2. Shall it recommend its members to join the League of
Women Voters?

3. Shall this be the last suffrage convention held under its
auspices? If not, when shall the next be called?

4. If this is to be the last convention, shall a Board of Officers be elected at this convention to serve until all tasks are
completed? If this is done, to whom shall such a board render its final report and by whom shall it be officially discharged?

5. If dissolution is determined upon, what disposition shall be made of (a) the files of data; (b) the property; (c) the funds, if any remain?

6. In the event that the association shall be dissolved what agency shall become the auxiliary of the International Woman Suffrage Alliance?

7. What plan for the intensive education of new women voters is possible and shall it be recommended that the League of Women Voters take up this work or shall it be conducted under the National American Woman Suffrage Association?

Victory in Sight

At the beginning of the afternoon session Mrs. Catt said that for twenty-eight years the Rev. Anna Howard Shaw had opened the national conventions with prayer and she asked that in memory of her the delegates rise and join in silent prayer. They did so and many were in tears. The Rev. Herbert L. Willet then offered the invocation. Mrs. Trout, president of the Illinois Suffrage Association, cordially welcomed the delegates to Chicago. . . . Mrs. Catt made a gracious response and resigning the chair to the first vice-president, Mrs. Katharine Dexter McCormick, gave a brief address, reserving a longer one for the League of Women Voters. She said in part:

> When we met at St. Louis a year ago in the 50th annual convention of our association, we knew that the end of our long struggle was near. We comprehended in a new sense the truth of [novelist] Victor Hugo's sage epigram: "There is one thing more powerful than Kings and Armies—the idea whose time has come to move." We knew that the time for our idea was here, and as State after State has joined the list of the ratified we have seen our idea, our cause, move forward dramatically, majestically into its appropriate place as part of the constitution of our nation. We have not yet the official proclamation announcing that our amendment has been ratified by the necessary thirty-six States, but thirty-one have done so and another will ratify before we adjourn; three Governors have promised special sessions very soon and two more

Legislatures will ratify when called together. There is no power on this earth that can do more than delay by a trifle the final enfranchisement of women.

The enemies of progress and liberty never surrender and never die. Ever since the days of cave-men they have stood ready with their sledge hammers to strike any liberal idea on the head whenever it appeared. They are still active, hysterically active, over our amendment; still imagining, as their progenitors for thousands of years have done, that a fly sitting on a wheel may command it to revolve no more and it will obey. They are running about from State to State, a few women and a few paid men. They dash to Washington to hold hurried consultations with senatorial friends and away to carry out instructions. . . . It does not matter. Suffragists were never dismayed when they were a tiny group and all the world was against them. What care they now when all the world is with them? March on, suffragists, the victory is yours! The trail has been long and winding; the struggle has been tedious and wearying; you have made sacrifices and received many hard knocks; be joyful to-day. Our final victory is due, is inevitable, is almost here. Let us celebrate to-day, and when the proclamation comes I beg you to celebrate the occasion with some form of joyous demonstration in your own home State. Two armistice days made a joyous ending of the war. Let two ratification days, one a National and one a State day, make a happy ending of the denial of political freedom to women!

Our amendment was submitted June 4, 1919, and to-day, eight months and eight days later, it has been ratified by thirty-one States. No other amendment made such a record but the time is not the significant part of the story. Of the thirty-one ratifications twenty-four have taken place in *special sessions.* These mean extra cost to the State, opportunity for other legislation and the chance of political intrigue for or against the Governor who calls them. These obstacles have been difficult to overcome, far more difficult than most of you will ever know, and in a few instances well-nigh insurmountable, but the point to emphasize to-day is that they *were* overcome. As a whole the ratifications have moved forward in splendid triumphal procession. There have been many inspiring incidents of daring and clever moves on the part of suffragists to speed the campaign and there have been many incidents of courage, nobility of purpose and proud scorn of the pettiness of political enemies on the part of Governors, legislators and men friends. On the other hand there have been tricks, chicanery and misrepresentation but let us forget them all. Victors can afford to be generous. . . .

We should be more than glad and grateful to-day, we should be proud—proud that our fifty-one years of organized endeavor have been clean, constructive, conscientious. Our association never resorted to lies, innuendoes, misrepresentation. It never accused its opponents of being free lovers, pro-Germans and Bolsheviki. It marched forward even when its forces were most disorganized by disaster. It always met argument with argument, honest objection with proof of error. In fifty years it never failed to send its representatives to plead our cause before every national political convention, although they went knowing that the prejudice they would meet was impregnable and the response would be ridicule and condemnation. It went to the rescue of every State campaign for half a century with such forces as it could command, even when realizing that there was no hope. In every corner it sowed the seeds of justice and trusted to time to bring the harvest. It has aided boys in high school with debates and later heard their votes of "yes" in Legislatures. Reporters assigned to our Washington conventions long, long ago, took their places at the press table on

Harry Burn's Mother Helps Ratify the Nineteenth Amendment

Sometimes important historical events rest on the actions of a small number of people—even one person can change the course of history. Historian Carole Bucy argues that such is the case of Harry Burn, Tennessee's youngest legislator in August 1920, when a note from his mother convinced him to vote in favor of ratifying the Nineteenth Amendment. In so doing, he helped Tennessee to become the thirty-sixth state to ratify the amendment. Thus, the Nineteenth Amendment, which gave American women the right to vote, became the supreme law of the land.

Harry Burn's one vote made the difference. The vote was 49 to 47. It seems that his mother back home had been reading the newspapers about the debate. So she wrote her son a note:

"Dear Son: Hurrah and vote for suffrage! I notice some

the first day with contempt and ridicule in their hearts but went out the last day won to our cause and later became editors of newspapers and spoke to thousands in our behalf. Girls came to our meetings, listened and accepted, and later as mature women became intrepid leaders.

In all the years this association has never paid a national lobbyist, and, so far as I know, no State has paid a legislative lobbyist. During the fifty years it has rarely had a salaried officer and even if so she has been paid less than her earning capacity elsewhere. It has been an army of volunteers who have estimated no sacrifice too great, no service too difficult.

Mrs. Catt enumerated some of the immortal pioneer suffragists and said: "How small seems the service of the rest of us by comparison, yet how glad and proud we have been to give it. Ours has been a cause to live for, a cause to die for if need be. It has been a movement with a soul, a dauntless, unconquerable soul ever leading onward. Women came, served and passed on but others took their places. . . .

of the speeches against. I have been watching to see how you stood but have not noticed anything. Don't forget to be a good boy and help Mrs. Catt put the 'rat' in ratification. Your Mother."

Young Harry Burn, whose decision had won voting rights for some 17 million women, was called upon to explain himself when the assembly reconvened the next day. He rose in the House chamber and said, "I know that a mother's advice is always safest for her boy to follow, and my mother wanted me to vote for ratification."

Burn had made up his mind that if the measure required only one extra vote, he would give it. After several unsuccessful attempts were made to stall the vote, the vote was taken. That letter was in Harry Burn's pocket and on his mind when he cast the decisive "aye" vote for ratification. Women had won by two votes, 49 to 47.

Carole Bucy, "Tennessee Women and the Vote: Tennessee's Pivotal Role in the Passage of the Nineteenth Amendment." www2.vscc.cc.tn.us/cbucy/History%202030/suffrage.htm.

How I pity the women who have had no share in the exaltation and the discipline of our army of workers! How I pity those who have not felt the grip of the oneness of women struggling, serving, suffering, sacrificing for the righteousness of women's emancipation! Oh, women, be glad today and let your voices ring out the gladness in your heart! There will never come another day like this. Let joy be unconfined and let it speak so clearly that its echo will be heard around the world and find its way into the soul of every woman of every race who is yearning for opportunity and liberty still denied. . . ."

President Wilson Congratulates the Association

After this inspiring address the convention was turned into a jollification meeting for a considerable time until the delegates were tired out by their enthusiasm and composed themselves to receive a telegram of greeting from President Woodrow Wilson addressed to Mrs. Catt: "Permit me to congratulate your association upon the fact that its great work is so near its triumphant end and that you can now merge it into a League of Women Voters to carry on the development of good citizenship and real democracy; and to wish for the new organization the same wise leadership and success." On motion of Mrs. McCormick it was voted that "the gratitude of the convention be expressed to the President for his constant cooperation and help, with deep regret for his illness." On motion of Miss Mary Garrett Hay, second vice-president, the convention authorized a letter of appreciation to be sent to the Governors of States that had ratified the Federal Amendment and telegrams to those who had not called special sessions strongly urging them to do so. This was made especially emphatic to Governor Louis F. Hart of Washington, the only equal suffrage State which had not ratified. [The session was called and the Legislature ratified unanimously March 22, leaving but one more to be gained.]

At the evening session the Recommendations were considered as presented by the Executive Council, which consisted of the president of the association, officers, board of directors, chairmen of standing and special committees, presidents of affiliated organizations and one representative of each society which paid dues on 1,500 or more members. After discussion and some amendment they were adopted as follows:

Whereas, The sole object of many years' endeavor by the National American Woman Suffrage Association has been "to secure the vote to the women citizens of the United States by appropriate national and State legislation" and that object is about to be attained, and

Whereas, The association must naturally dissolve or take up new lines of work when the last suffrage task has been completed, therefore, be it

Resolved, That the association shall assume no new lines of work and shall move toward dissolution by the following process:

(1) That a Board of Officers shall be elected at this convention, as usual, to serve two years (if necessary) in accordance with the provisions of the constitution;

(2) That the eight directors elected at the 50th annual convention, and whose term of office does not expire until March, 1921, shall be asked to serve until the term of elected officers shall expire;

(3) That any vacancy or vacancies occurring in the list of directors shall be filled by election at this convention;

(4) That all vacancies in the Board of Directors occurring after this convention shall be filled by majority vote of the board;

(5) That the Board of Officers so constituted shall have full charge of the remainder of the ratification campaign and all necessary legal proceedings and shall dispose of files, books, data, property and funds (if any remain) of the association subject to the further instruction of this convention. The Executive Council shall be subject to call by the Board of Officers if necessary;

(6) That the Board of Officers shall render a quarterly account of its procedure and an annual report of all funds in its possession duly audited by certified accountant, to the women who in February, 1920, compose its Executive Council. When its work is completed and its final report has been accepted by this council it may by formal resolution dissolve.

A resolution was adopted regarding action in case of a referendum to the voters of ratification by a Legislature but later the U.S. Supreme Court declared this unconstitutional. Another urged the new league to make political education of the voters its first duty. The last resolution was as follows:

"We recommend that the League of Women Voters, now a section of the National American Women Suffrage Association, be organized as a new and independent society, and that its auxiliaries, while retaining their relationship to the Board of Officers to be elected in this 51st convention in form, shall change their names, objects and constitutions to conform to those of the National League of Women Voters and take up the plan of work to be adopted by its first congress."

Chronology

1838
Kentucky gives widows with school-aged children the right to vote in school elections.

1840
Elizabeth Cady Stanton and Lucretia Mott, two members of the American delegation to the World Anti-Slavery Convention held in London, England, are denied the opportunity to participate because of their gender; being excluded from the meetings, they vow to hold a separate conference to address the unequal rights of women.

1848
Stanton and Mott hold the first conference on women's rights in Stanton's hometown of Seneca Falls, New York; the convention produces a document, the Declaration of Sentiments, which serves as the foundation for the women's rights movement for decades; the most controversial element is a call for women's suffrage.

1861
Kansas grants women the right to vote in school board elections.

1868
The Fourteenth Amendment to the U.S. Constitution is adopted; this amendment introduces the word *male* into the Constitution for the first time.

1869
The women's suffrage movement splits over whether a national or state-by-state battle for women's suffrage would

be more effective; Stanton and Susan B. Anthony form the liberal National Woman Suffrage Association (NWSA), which fights for a national solution; Henry Blackwell and Lucy Stone start the more conservative American Woman Suffrage Association (AWSA), which advocates state-level changes; the Wyoming Territory grants women the right to vote.

1870

The Fifteenth Amendment is ratified; this amendment officially reaffirms the rights of male former slaves to vote; this distinction suggests that it will probably take a separate amendment to enfranchise women.

1872

Anthony, Virginia Minor, and other prominent supporters of women's suffrage attempt to vote in U.S. presidential elections; they argue that nothing in the Constitution explicitly prohibits women from voting; furthermore, since the Fourtheenth Amendment creates national citizenship and since voting is a critical property of democratic citizenship, they argue that women have the constitutional right to vote.

1873

Anthony, denied the ability to speak on her behalf during her trial, is fined one hundred dollars for illegally voting in the 1872 presidential election; she refuses to pay the fine, and no further legal action is taken against her.

1875

The U.S. Supreme Court unanimously rules in *Minor v. Happersett* that individual states are allowed to restrict women from voting; this implies that the women's suffrage movement will either have to convince each state to adopt female enfranchisement or secure the passage of a constitutional amendment that grants all American women the right to vote.

1887

Kansas grants women the right to vote in municipal elections.

1890

The NWSA and the AWSA merge into one organization, the National American Woman Suffrage Association (NAWSA); Stanton is named NAWSA's first president; upon statehood, Wyoming becomes the first state to allow women the right to vote.

1893

Colorado becomes the first state in which women are granted the right to vote by a statewide referendum.

1896

Utah and Idaho both vote to enfranchise women.

1910

The state of Washington grants female enfranchisement.

1911

California gives women the right to vote.

1912

Oregon, Kansas, and Arizona grant women the right to vote.

1913

Illinois becomes the first state east of the Mississippi River to give women the right to vote; the day before Woodrow Wilson is inaugurated as president of the United States, Alice Paul organizes a suffrage parade through the streets of Washington, D.C.; although she gathered the appropriate permits for the parade and the District of Columbia police pledged to help with crowd management during the parade, the marchers faced significant harassment by some members of the crowd and even by the police officers; hearings were held in Congress to determine if the police had been derelict in their duties; the officers were exonerated, yet several members of the U.S. Senate reprimanded the police force for failing to protect the parade participants.

1917
New York State passes a full suffrage state constitutional amendment by referendum.

1918
January 10: The House of Representatives approves the Nineteenth Amendment by a vote of 274 to 136, precisely the two-thirds majority that is needed to propose an amendment.

September 30: President Wilson challenges political convention by personally urging the U.S. Senate to vote in favor of the Nineteenth Amendment.

October 1: Irritated by the president's interference and believing that the federal government should not dictate to the states whether women should be allowed to vote, the Senate narrowly rejects, by a vote of sixty-two in favor and thirty-four opposed, the Nineteenth Amendment, two votes shy of the necessary two-thirds majority.

1919
May 20: The U.S. House of Representatives, by an overwhelming vote of 304 to 89, approves the Nineteenth Amendment.

June 5: The U.S. Senate passes the Nineteenth Amendment by the necessary two-thirds majority; the amendment is officially proposed and moves to the states for their ratification.

June 10: Wisconsin and Illinois, whose legislatures are in session at the time, both ratify the Nineteenth Amendment; although Illinois technically finished its voting first, the clerk had made an error in writing the ratification order;

therefore, Wisconsin is officially credited with being the first state to ratify the amendment.

1920

August 18: Harry Burn, Tennessee's youngest legislator, takes the advice of his mother and votes in favor of ratifying the Nineteenth Amendment; his vote helps ensure that Tennessee becomes the thirty-sixth state to ratify the amendment.

November: The first elections in which all American women over the age of twenty-one are legally allowed to vote occur.

For Further Research

Frances M. Björkman and Annie G. Porritt, eds., *"The Blue Book": Woman Suffrage—History, Arguments, and Results*. New York: National Woman Suffrage, 1917.

Harriot Stanton Blatch and Alma Lutz, *Challenging Years: The Memoirs of Harriot Stanton Blatch*. New York: G.P. Putnam's Sons, 1940.

Carole Bucy, "Tennessee Women and the Vote: Tennessee's Pivotal Role in the Passage of the Nineteenth Amendment," Unpublished manuscript. www2.vscc.cc.tn.us.

Mari Jo Buhle and Paul Buhle, eds., *The Concise History of Woman Suffrage: Selections from the Classic Work of Stanton, Anthony, Gage, and Harper*. Urbana: University of Illinois Press, 1978.

Carrie Chapman Catt and Nettie Rogers Shuler, *Woman Suffrage and Politics*. New York: Charles Scribner's Sons, 1923.

Ellen DuBois, *Feminism and Suffrage: The Emergence of an Independent Women's Movement in America, 1848–1869*. Ithaca, NY: Cornell University Press, 1978.

Ellen DuBois, ed., *The Elizabeth Cady Stanton–Susan B. Anthony Reader*. Boston: Northeastern University Press, 1992.

Abigail Scott Duniway, *Path Breaking: An Autobiographical History of the Equal Suffrage Movement in Pacific Coast States*. New York: Source Book, 1970.

Margaret Finnegan, *Selling Suffrage: Consumer Culture and Votes for Women*. New York: Columbia University Press, 1999.

Eleanor Flexnor, *Century of Struggle: The Woman's Rights Movement in the United States*. New York: Atheneum, 1972.

Sherna Gluck, ed., *From Parlor to Prison: Five American Suffragists Talk About Their Lives*. New York: Vintage Books, 1976.

Ann D. Gordon, "Elizabeth Cady Staton and the Woman's Rights Movement," in *American Reform and Reformers: A Biographical Dictionary*. Ed. Randall M. Miller and Paul A. Cimbala. Westport, CT: Greenwood, 1996.

Sara Hunter Graham, *Woman Suffrage and the New Democracy*. New Haven, CT: Yale University Press, 1996.

Alan P. Grimes, *The Puritan Ethic and Woman Suffrage*. New York: Oxford University Press, 1967.

Miriam Gurko, *The Ladies of Seneca Falls*. New York: Macmillan, 1974.

J.A. Haien, ed., *Anti-Suffrage Essays*. Boston: Forum Publications of Boston, 1916.

Ida Husted Harper, ed., *The Life and Work of Susan B. Anthony*. Vol. 2. Indianapolis: Bowen Merrill, 1898.

Inez Haynes Irwin, *The Story of the Woman's Party*. New York: Harcourt Brace, 1921.

Thomas J. Jablonsky, *The Home, Heaven, and Mother Party: Female Anti-Suffragists in the United States, 1868–1920*. Brooklyn, NY: Carlson, 1994.

Aileen S. Kraditor, *The Ideas of the Woman Suffrage Movement, 1890–1920*. New York: Columbia University Press, 1965.

Gerda Lerner, ed., *The Female Experience: An American Documentary*. New York: Oxford University Press, 1977.

Susan E. Marshall, *Splintered Sisterhood: Gender and Class in the Campaign Against Woman Suffrage*. Madison: University of Wisconsin Press, 1997.

Nancy McGlen et al., *Women, Politics, and American Society*. 3rd ed. New York: Longman, 2002.

David Morgan, *Suffragists and Democrats*. East Lansing: Michigan State University Press, 1972.

National American Woman Suffrage Association, *How Women Won It*. New York: H.W. Wilson, 1940.

Mary Beth Norton, ed., *Major Problems in American Women's History*. Lexington, MA: D.C. Heath, 1989.

Maud Wood Park, *Front Door Lobby*. Boston: Beacon, 1960.

Ross Evan Paulson, *Women's Suffrage and Prohibition*. Glenview: Scott, Foresman, 1973.

Mary Gray Peck, *Carrie Chapman Catt*. New York: H.W. Wilson, 1944.

Mary P. Ryan, *Womanhood in America*. 3rd ed. New York: Franklin Watts, 1983.

Anne Scott and Andrew Scott, eds., *One Half the People: The Fight for Woman Suffrage*. Philadelphia: J.B. Lippincott, 1975.

Anna Howard Shaw, *The Story of a Pioneer*. New York: Harper and Brothers, 1915.

Andrew Sinclair, *The Emancipation of the American Woman*. New York: Harper and Row, 1966.

Elizabeth Cady Stanton, Susan B. Anthony, and Matilda Joslyn Gage, eds., *History of Woman Suffrage*. 6 vols. New York: Arno, 1969.

Doris Stevens, *Jailed for Freedom*. Freeport, NY: Books for Libraries, 1920.

Sylvia Strauss, *"Traitors to the Masculine Cause": The Men's Campaigns for Women's Rights*. Westport, CT: Greenwood, 1982.

Woman's Rights Conventions: Seneca Falls and Rochester, 1848. New York: Arno and the New York Times, 1969.

Index